ALASKAN
HALIBUT
RECIPES

By CECILIA NIBECK

AK Enterprises
Anchorage, Alaska

ALASKAN HALIBUT RECIPES

By Cecilia Nibeck

Copyright © 1989, 1996 and 2002 by Stuart Nibeck

**P.O. Box 210241
Anchorage, AK 99521-0241**

Acknowledgements

ILLUSTRATIONS
Barbara Lavallee, an Alaskan artist represented
by Artique, Ltd., 314 G Street, Anchorage, Alaska

PUBLISHING CONSULTANT
Rainforest Publishing, Anchorage, Alaska

ISBN # 0-9622117-0-2
Printed in the U.S.A.

10 9 8 7 6 5

PREFACE

Few Alaskans hesitate to enjoy the bounty of the world around them. Our state is known for its abundance of fish and game, and we relish our ability to regularly dine on delectables that others elsewhere taste only occasionally.

Every Alaskan cook has that special fish or game recipe that's been developed meal by meal, year by year, until it is just right. That recipe is often handed down from generation to generation until it becomes a part of a family's lore. The recipes in this book are part of many families' lore.

Two years ago we published our first cookbook, *Salmon Recipes*. The success of that project proved to us that a simple book containing simple but noteworthy recipes using Alaskans' most chosen fish species could be worthwhile both in the book-stores and in the kitchen, and we pledged to do another.

Our newest book, *Alaskan Halibut Recipes,* is, like its prede-cessor, a collection of recipes from our family and our friends. Its simplicity speaks to our belief that the best cooks require only a recipe to send them on the path to culinary adventure. We leave cluttersome tables and charts to other cookbooks; we offer only recipes--good recipes.

We thank all of those who contributed their time and exper-tise to the recipes in this book, and we hope that the cooks who use these recipes appreciate the special qualities of those who created them.

Cecilia and Stu Nibeck
AK Enterprises
April 1, 1989

Table of Contents

Soups and Appetizers

Main Courses

SOUPS AND APPETIZERS

Levallee © 1988

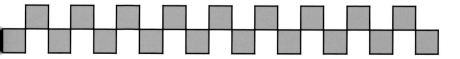

POTATO
HALIBUT CHOWDER

2 lbs. halibut fillets, cut into 1-inch cubes
3 cups water
4 medium potatoes, cut into 1/2-inch cubes
1 large onion, chopped
1 medium green pepper, chopped
1 tomato, peeled and chopped
1 cup cream or half and half
1-3/4 tsps. salt
1/4 tsp. pepper
1/3 cup cheddar cheese, shredded

❖

Add halibut to boiling water. Cover and simmer about 10 minutes. Separate halibut and broth. Simmer potatoes, onions and peppers in a cup of the broth until potatoes are tender. Stir in the rest of the broth, halibut, tomatoes, cream and pepper. Heat until hot. Sprinkle with cheese. Serves six.

ANCHORAGE HALIBUT CHOWDER

2 lbs. halibut fillets
1/4 lb. salt pork, diced
2 large onions, diced
small amount of cayenne pepper
1/2 tsp. nutmeg
6 pilot biscuits, broken into pieces
2 tbsp. catsup
1 cup sherry

❖

Saute pork and onions until brown. Put halibut in large pan. Add pork, onions, seasoning and biscuits. Cover and cook for 55 minutes. Add catsup and wine. Serves four.

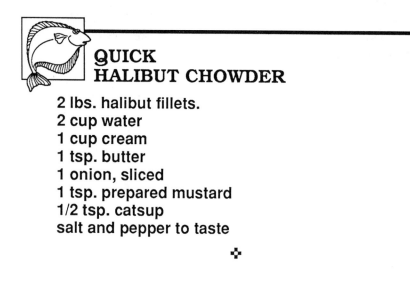

QUICK HALIBUT CHOWDER

2 lbs. halibut fillets.
2 cup water
1 cup cream
1 tsp. butter
1 onion, sliced
1 tsp. prepared mustard
1/2 tsp. catsup
salt and pepper to taste

❖

Boil fillets in water until tender. Chop halibut into small pieces. Reduce heat and add remaining ingredients. Simmer slowly until thick. Season to taste. Serves four.

FISH CHOWDER

1 lb. halibut fillets, cut into 1-inch cubes
1 tbsp. butter
2 cups diced, cubed potatoes
2 cups sliced cubed carrots
2 cups sliced onions
2 whole cloves
1 tbsp. snipped fresh dill or 1 tsp. dried dillweed
1 bay leaf
Salt to taste
2 cups boiling water
1/2 cup dry white wine
2 tbsp. flour
1 cup skim or low-fat milk
pepper to taste
2 tbsp. finely chopped parsley

❖

Melt butter in 6 quart saucepan. Add potatoes, carrots, onions, cloves, dill, bay leaf and salt, and boiling water. Simmer, covered, 20 minutes.

Add fish and wine. Simmer, covered, 10 minutes.

Stir together flour and milk in small bowl until smooth. Stir into soup. Cook, stirring, until slightly thickened. Season with pepper. Sprinkle each serving with parsley. Serves six.

HALIBUT CHOWDER

1 lb. halibut fillets, cut into 1-inch cubes
3 slices bacon, diced
1 large onion, finely chopped
2 cloves garlic, minced
1/2 green pepper, seeded and chopped
1 large can (48 oz.) chicken broth
1 bay leaf
1/2 tsp. parsley flakes
1/8 tsp. pepper
1/4 cup long grain rice

❖

Fry bacon until crisp. Lift out and set aside. Add onion and garlic to bacon drippings and saute until limp. Stir in green pepper, broth, bay leaf, parsley and pepper. Bring to boil. Add rice and cover. Simmer for 10 minutes.

Add halibut to broth after rice has cooked for 10 minutes. Continue to simmer until rice is tender and fish flakes readily. Stir in bacon and serve. Makes 4 servings.

SEAFOOD
CHOWDER

1 lb. halibut fillets, cut into 1-inch cubes
2 slices bacon, chopped
1/2 cup onion, chopped
2 cups water
1 cup potato, diced
2 cups milk
1 tsp. salt
Dash pepper

❖

    Fry bacon until crisp. Add onion and cook until tender. Add water and potatoes and simmer 10 minutes or until potatoes are partially tender. Add halibut and simmer until potatoes and halibut are tender. Add milk and seasonings. Heat thoroughly and serve immediately. Serves six.

FISH
CHOWDER

1 lb. halibut, cut into 1-inch cubes
1 medium onion, chopped
1 large carrot, sliced thin
1/2 cup celery, finely diced
1 clove garlic, crushed (optional)
2 tbsp. butter
1 can (6-1/2 oz.) clams, minced
3 cups chicken broth
1 can (8-1/4 oz.) stewed tomatoes
1 bay leaf
1/2 tsp. leaf thyme
Dash of cayenne
Salt to taste

❖

Saute onion, carrot, celery and garlic in butter until onion is tender. Drain liquid from clams into pan. Add broth, tomatoes, bay leaf, thyme and cayenne. Bring to boil. Cover and simmer 15 minutes. Add halibut and bring to boil again. Cover and simmer until fish flakes easily. Add clams and salt. Remove bay leaf. Makes about 6 cups.

HALIBUT CHOWDER

1 lb. halibut, cut into 1-inch cubes
1 can condensed cream of potato soup
1 tsp. onion powder
1/2 tsp. salt
1/4 tsp. thyme
1/4 tsp. pepper
1 can (16 oz.) tomatoes, cut up
1 can (16 oz.) mixed vegetables

❖

Place large size (14" x 20") Oven Cooking Bag in 3-quart casserole. Combine all ingredients in bag turning bag several times to mix. Close bag with nylon tie. Make 6 half-inch slits in top near closure. Bake at 350° until fish flakes easily. Serves four.

HALIBUT
VEGETABLE CHOWDER

1 lb. halibut, cut into 1-inch cubes
2 carrots, cut in thin julienne strips
2 stalks celery, sliced diagonally
1/2 cup onion, chopped
1 clove garlic, minced
2 tbsp. oil
1 can (28 oz.) tomatoes
1 cup water
3 tbsp. minced parsley, divided
1 tsp. chicken bouillon granules
1/4 tsp. each thyme and basil leaves, crushed

✢

Saute carrots, celery, onion and garlic in oil for 5 minutes. Add tomatoes, water, 2 tbsp. parsley, bouillon and seasonings. Break up tomatoes with spoon. Cover and simmer 20 minutes. Add halibut to chowder. Cover and simmer until halibut flakes easily. Sprinkle with remaining parsley. Serves six.

HALIBUT-CORN CHOWDER

1 lb. halibut, cut into 1-inch cubes
2 slices bacon, diced
1 small onion, chopped
1 tbsp. flour
1 medium potato, peeled and diced
1 cup water
Salt and pepper
1/8 tsp. dillweed
1 can (8 oz.) whole-kernel corn, undrained
1 cup half-and-half
1 cup milk
2 tbsp. chopped parsley

❖

Cook bacon in kettle until crisp. Remove bacon; drain and set aside. Saute onion in fat remaining in kettle until tender. Stir in flour. Add potato, water, salt, pepper and dillweed. Bring to boil. Cover and simmer until potato is tender. Add halibut. Cover and simmer until fish flakes easily. Add corn, half-and-half and milk. Heat gently, but do not boil. Add salt and pepper to taste. Sprinkle with reserved bacon and parsley. Serves four.

BASQUE HALIBUT STEW

1 lb. halibut fillet
1/4 cup olive oil
1-1/2 cup onions, chopped
2 tbsp. garlic, minced
1-1/2 cup tomatoes, chopped
Pepper to taste

✤

Saute onion and garlic in olive oil for three minutes. Add halibut. Cover and simmer 25 minutes. Add tomatoes. Cover and simmer until halibut flakes easily. Season and serve with rice or small boiled potatoes. Serves six.

CREOLE HALIBUT STEW

2 lbs. halibut, cut into 1-inch cubes
2 onions, minced
1 green pepper, minced
6 celery ribs, minced
4 tbsp. butter
1 (14-16 oz.) can tomatoes, chopped
2 (6 oz.) cans tomato paste
3/4 cup water
1/4 lemon, thinly sliced
1 garlic clove, minced
1 tbsp. salt

Saute onions, green pepper and celery in butter. Add tomatoes, tomato paste, water, lemon slices, garlic and salt. Cook very slowly for two hours. Add fish and cook without stirring for 20 minutes. Pour over cooked rice in deep bowls. Serves four.

RUSSIAN SEAFOOD STEW

2 lbs. halibut, cut into 1-inch cubes
2 cups onions, sliced
1/2 cup olive oil
3 cups fresh tomatoes, chopped
2 cups canned Italian plum tomatoes
8 cloves garlic, chopped
1/2 tsp. thyme
1/4 tsp. fennel seeds
1/4 tsp. turmeric
1 quart water
1 quart chicken broth
1 large dungeness crab, cracked
1 quart clams

❖

Saute onion in oil for 5 minutes. Add remaining ingredients except halibut, crab and clams, and cover. Simmer for 45 minutes.

Strain, pressing juices out of ingredients. Add clams and crab. Simmer for five minutes. Add halibut and cook until halibut is opaque. Serves six.

HALIBUT STEW
WITH DUMPLINGS

1-1/2 lbs. halibut, cut into 1-inch cubes
1 cup carrots, sliced
1/2 cup onion, chopped
1/2 cup celery, sliced
2 tbsp. vegetable oil
2 tbsp. baking mix
1-1/2 cups water
1/2 cup dry white wine
1/2 tsp. instant chicken bouillon granules
1/4 tsp. salt
1/4 tsp. dried dill weed
1 cup frozen green peas
1/4 cup green pepper, chopped
1 cup baking mix
1/3 cup milk
2 tbsp. parsley, snipped

❖

Saute carrots, onion and celery in oil in skillet until onion is tender. Thoroughly mix in 2 tbsp. baking mix. Stir in water, wine, bouillon (dry), salt and dill weed. Heat to simmering; simmer uncovered 15 minutes.

Stir halibut, peas and green pepper into vegetable mixture. Mix one cup baking mix, milk and parsley, until soft dough forms. Heat halibut mixture to boiling over medium heat. Drop dough by six spoonfuls onto boiling halibut mixture. Reduce heat. Simmer uncovered 10 minutes. Cover and simmer 10 minutes longer. Serves four to six

SUNSET STEW

1 lb. halibut, cut into 1-inch cubes
2 tbsp. butter
1 medium onion, chopped
4 cups chicken broth
1 cup dry white wine
2 medium-sized potatoes, cut into 1-inch chunks
1 bay leaf
1/2 tsp. fennel seed
Salt to taste
Pepper to taste

❖

Saute onion in butter until soft. Add chicken broth, wine, bay leaf, and fennel seed. Bring to a boil, cover, and simmer until potatoes are tender. Add halibut and cover. Simmer until fish flakes easily. Salt and pepper to taste. Serves four.

GREAT
AUTUMN STEW

2 lbs. halibut fillet, cut into 1-inch cubes
Salt and pepper
Juice of 1 lemon
3 onions, chopped coarse
2 cloves garlic, minced
1/4 cup minced parsley
1/4 cup olive oil
1/2 cup dry white wine
1 large (28-oz) can tomatoes, chopped
1 tsp. rubbed oregano

❖

Marinate halibut in lemon juice and season with salt and pepper. Set aside.

In a large oven-proof skillet, saute onion, garlic, and parsley in olive oil until vegetables are tender. Add wine and cook several minutes. Add tomatoes, heat to a boil. Add oregano, salt, pepper and halibut. Put skillet in 350° oven. Bake until fish is cooked. Serves four.

SIBERIAN STEW

1-1/2 lbs. halibut fillets, cut into 1-inch cubes
1 lb. fresh mushrooms, sliced
3/4 cup onion, sliced
1/4 cup butter
1 (16 oz) can tomatoes
1 (4 oz.) can clams with juice
1/2 cup diced dill pickles
1 tsp. salt
1/4 tsp. pepper
1/4 cup fresh parsley, chopped
6 whole, boiled potatoes

❖

Saute mushrooms and onion in butter for 3 or 4 minutes. Add tomatoes, clams with juice, pickles, salt, and pepper. Bring to a boil. Add halibut and reduce heat. Cover and simmer until fish is done. Stir in parsley. Serve in a soup bowl over a whole, boiled potato. Serves six.

SCANDINAVIAN
HALIBUT SOUP

2 lbs. halibut, cooked and flaked
1 cup onion, chopped
1/2 cup green pepper, chopped
3 tbsp. olive oil
1 can (16 oz.) tomatoes
2 cups lima beans, drained
1 bottle (8 oz.) clam juice
2 cups chicken broth
2 tsp. salt
1/4 tsp. pepper
1/4 cup parsley, chopped

❖

Saute onions and green pepper in olive oil. Add tomatoes and simmer for ten minutes. Add lima beans, tomato mixture, and clam juice to the chicken broth. Bring to a boil. Add halibut and heat. Season and sprinkle with parsley. Serves six.

HEARTWARMING HALIBUT SOUP

1-1/2 lbs. halibut, cut into 1-inch cubes
2 tbsp. olive oil or salad oil
1 large onion, chopped
1 clove garlic, minced or mashed
1 cup thinly sliced celery
1 can (1 lb. 12 oz.) tomatoes
2 cans (about 14 oz. each) regular-strength
  chicken broth
1/4 tsp. each oregano, basil,
  and rosemary leaves
1/3 cup rice
1 package (9 oz.) frozen Italian green beans
2 tbsp. chopped parsley
Freshly grated Parmesan cheese

✣

Heat oil in a 5-quart kettle over medium heat. Add onion, garlic, and celery. Saute until onion is limp. Stir in tomatoes (break up with a spoon) and their liquid, broth, oregano, basil, rosemary, and rice. Cover and simmer for 10 minutes. Add beans and simmer, covered, until rice and beans are cooked.

Add halibut and simmer until fish flakes easily. Sprinkle with parsley and Parmesan cheese. Makes 6 servings.

HALIBUT TOMATO SOUP

1 lb. halibut fillets, cut into 1-inch cubes
1/4 cup bacon, chopped
1/2 cup onion, chopped
1/2 cup celery, chopped
2 cups water
1-1/2 tsp. salt
Dash pepper
1/3 cup rice uncooked
2 cups tomato juice

❖

Fry bacon until crisp. Add onion and celery and cook until tender. Add water, seasonings and rice. Simmer 10 minutes. Add fish and simmer until rice and fish are tender. Add tomato juice and heat thoroughly. Serves six.

ORIENTAL FISH SOUP

8 oz. cooked halibut, broken into small pieces
5 oz. mild ground miso
8 oz. tofu, diced
5 cups chicken broth
2 leeks, sliced

❖

Mix everything but leeks and bring to a boil. Add leeks and serve. Serves six.

FRENCH
HALIBUT SOUP

4 lbs. halibut fillet, cut into 1-inch cubes
2 tbsp. olive oil
1 onion, chopped
2 celery ribs, chopped
4 raw potatoes, diced
2 tomatoes, chopped
1 small garlic clove, minced
Sprig of fresh fennel
3 cups dry white wine
1 tsp. salt
1/4 tsp. pepper
Pinch of saffron

❖

Saute onion and celery in oil. Add remaining ingredients. Simmer until tender, about 10 minutes. Serves six.

NEW ENGLAND HALIBUT CHOWDER

12 oz. halibut fillet, cut into 1-inch cubes
1 can (11 oz.) cream of potato soup
1 (2-3/4 oz) package leek soup mix
1 cup water
1/4 cup dry white wine
2 cups milk
1 tbsp. lemon juice
1/8 tsp. pepper
Parsley

❖

Combine potato soup with leek soup in large sauce pan. Stir in 1 cup water. Add wine. Bring to a boil, stirring often. Add fish to soup mixture. Simmer 3 to 5 minutes. Add milk, lemon juice and pepper. Reheat to steaming. If soup seems too thick, thin with a little more milk. Garnish with fresh parsley. Serves four.

CREAMY
HALIBUT SOUP

1-1/2 lbs. halibut fillets, cut into 1-inch chunks
3 tbsp. olive oil
1 tbsp. minced garlic
1 cup minced onion
2 tsp. crumbled whole saffron
1/2 tsp. chopped fresh or dried thyme
3 drops Tabasco
1/2 tsp. salt
1/8 tsp. freshly ground pepper
1 cup dry white wine
4 cups water
1/3 cup tomato puree
1 tsp. crushed fennel seeds
3 tbsp. Cognac
2 cups heavy cream

❖

Saute garlic, onion, saffron and thyme in oil until onion is wilted. Add fish, and season with Tabasco, salt and pepper. Add wine, water, tomato puree and fennel seeds. Bring to boil and simmer for 15 minutes, stirring occasionally.

Add Cognac, stir in cream, and bring to a boil. Simmer for 10 minutes. Serves eight.

THAI HALIBUT PUDDING

1-1/2 lbs. halibut fillets, ground very fine
2 tbsp. shrimp or anchovy paste
1-1/2 cups coconut milk
4 tbsp. minced scallions
2 tbsp. cabbage, grated
1 tbsp. garlic, minced
1 tsp. lemon rind, grated
1/2 tsp. dried ground chile pepper
Salt and pepper to taste
1 egg
1/2 cup heavy cream

❖

Blend ground fish with shrimp paste, coconut milk and remaining ingredients except egg and cream. Season with salt and pepper to taste. Beat for a few minutes; then beat in the egg. Divide among 6 individual baking dishes. Spoon cream on top and cover with foil. Set in a pan of hot water. Bake at 325° for 1 hour, or until set. Serves six.

HALIBUT SOUP
WITH FISH BALLS

3 lbs. trimmings, head, and bones
   of a 6-10 lb. halibut
3 quarts water
1 large onion, chopped
1 cup celery, with leaves
1 carrot, grated
2 cloves garlic, minced
2 tbsp. oil
1 bay leaf
10 peppercorns
1/3 cup tomato sauce
1 tsp. rubbed oregano
Salt and pepper to taste
Cheesecloth

❖

    Wrap fish trimmings in cheesecloth and place in a large kettle with 3 quarts of cold water. Saute onions, celery, carrot, and garlic in oil until tender. Add vegetables, bay leaf and peppercorns to stock and simmer for 30 minutes. Strain stock, discard solids, then return stock to a clean kettle. Add tomato sauce, oregano, and salt and pepper. Simmer slowly while making fish balls. Serves six.

Instructions for fish balls are on the following page.

FISH BALLS

1 lb. boned, ground halibut
Salt and pepper to taste
1 egg beaten
1/2 cup cornstarch
1/4 tsp. rubbed oregano

❖

Season ground fish with salt and pepper, beat in egg, cornstarch, and oregano. When smooth, chill for 1 hour. Form fish into walnut-size balls, drop them into boiling broth, and simmer for 20 minutes.

ALMOND HALIBUT SOUP

1/2 lb. halibut fillets
1 medium onion, sliced
4 peppercorns
1 tbsp. fennel seeds
1/4 cup dry white wine
1/3 cup blanched almonds
1/4 cup sour cream
Fresh dill, chopped

Poach fillets, onion, peppercorns, fennel seeds, in white wine and enough water to cover them. When halibut flakes easily, remove it from the liquid. Place halibut and almonds in a blender with strained cooking liquid. Blend until smooth. Strain to remove any fine bones. Return to a clean saucepan and reheat. Stir in sour cream. Pour into hot soup bowls. Sprinkle with dill. Serves four.

SAFFRON HALIBUT SOUP

1-1/2 lbs. halibut fillets, cut into 1-inch cubes
1 head fennel, finely chopped
3 medium onions
1 clove garlic
2 tbsp. oil
Salt and pepper to taste
1 bay leaf
1/2 tsp. dried thyme
1/2 cup white wine
2-1/2 cups water
Dash powdered saffron
Large strip orange rind

❖

Saute fennel, onions and garlic in oil until soft but not browned. Season with salt and pepper. Add bay leaf, thyme and wine. Add fish, water, saffron and orange rind. Cook over slow heat covered for 45 minutes. Remove orange rind and bay leaf and serve hot. Serves four.

HALIBUT SOUP
WITH GRUYERE

2 lbs. halibut, cut into 1-inch cubes
1/3 cup olive oil
1/2 tsp. salt
1/4 tsp. pepper
1 quart milk
3 tbsp. olive oil
2 large onions, chopped
1 (32 oz.) can Italian plum tomatoes, peeled
1/4 tsp. dried basil
1/4 lb. very thin spaghetti
6 oz. Gruyere cheese, grated

❖

Heat 1/3 cup olive oil in large pan over medium flame until hot. Add fish, salt, and pepper. Heat for about 5 minutes. Add milk. Lower heat and simmer for 30 minutes. Saute onions in 3 tbsp. oil until they are translucent. Add tomatoes and basil and cook for 15 minutes. Add tomato mixture to the soup pot. Continue cooking for 20 minutes.

A half hour before serving, heat soup to boiling. Add spaghetti, broken up, and cook until tender (about 15 minutes). Before serving, sprinkle Gruyere in the center of each serving of soup. Serves six.

FISH SOUP
EXOTICA

2 lbs. halibut fillets
1 tsp. salt
2-3 green (unripe) bananas, sliced in rounds
1 yellow onion, sliced
4 tbsp. olive oil
2 cloves garlic
1 bay leaf
1 chili pepper or 1/2 tsp. cayenne pepper
1 bunch parsley, finely chopped
2 large tomatoes, chopped
1/4 cup tapioca
1/4 cup dry bread crumbs
1/2 of a small cabbage, chopped
4-6 large potatoes, chopped in chunks
4-6 sweet potatoes, chopped in chunks

✣

Dissolve salt in enough water to cover banana pieces and soak for 10-15 minutes.

Saute onion in oil. Add garlic, bay leaf, pepper, parsley and tomato, and saute for several minutes, stirring frequently. Stir in 4 cups hot water. Bring soup almost to a boil. Add tapioca and bread crumbs, stirring vigorously. Immediately reduce heat to simmer. Drain bananas and add them, along with the cabbage and potatoes. Gently lay in the fish, cover with water, and simmer for 20-30 minutes, or until everything is done. Serves six.

ITALIAN
FISH SOUP

2 lbs. halibut, cut into 1-inch cubes
2 garlic cloves, crushed
1/4 cup olive oil
3 cups water
1 tbsp. fennel tops, chopped
1 tbsp. parsley, chopped
1/2 tsp. dried oregano
Pinch of Italian red pepper

❖

Saute garlic in oil for 1 minute. Add remaining ingredients. Simmer until halibut is tender. Salt to taste. Serves four.

SCANDINAVIAN
DILLED HALIBUT SALAD

1-1/2 cup cooked halibut, flaked
4 red skinned potatoes, cooked and sliced
4 tomatoes, sliced and peeled
1 red onion, sliced
6 tbsp. olive oil
2 tbsp. tarragon vinegar
1/4 tsp. prepared mustard
Salt and pepper
Dill
1 tbsp. capers, chopped

In a deep salad bowl, alternate layers of halibut, potatoes, onions, tomatoes and capers. Make a dressing of oil, vinegar and mustard; add salt and pepper. Toss salad with dressing, chill. Garnish with dill. Serves four.

GREAT
HALIBUT SALAD

2 cups cooked halibut, flaked
1-1/2 cups boiling water
1/2 tsp. salt
1 cup diced celery
1 cup mayonnaise
2 packages lemon-flavored Jello
1/4 cup vinegar
1 cup carrot, grated
1/4 cup green pepper, chopped
4 green onions, chopped fine
Lettuce

❖

Dissolve Jello in boiling water. Add vinegar and salt. Chill until almost congealed. Fold in carrot, celery, green onion, green pepper, mayonnaise and fish. Place in molds, chill until firm. Unmold on lettuce. Serves six.

HALIBUT
CEVICHE SALAD

3/4 lb. boneless halibut, cut into 1/4-inch cubes
1/2 lb. small shrimp, cooked and shelled
1/2 lb. scallops, thinly sliced
1/2 cup freshly squeezed lime juice
4 large tomatoes
2 cups green onions, chopped (with some tops)
1/2 cup white wine vinegar
1/2 cup tomato-based chili sauce
1/2 cup fresh coriander (cilantro),
   coarsely chopped
1/3 cup olive oil
1/3 cup red or green salsa jalapeno
1/4 cup dry white wine
1 tsp. oregano leaves
Salt and pepper
Lime wedges

❖

    In a small, deep bowl, place halibut, scallops, and lime juice. Mix well. Cover and chill at least 3 hours until fish turns an opaque white. Stir occasionally. Drain and discard liquid. Peel and core 4 large tomatoes and cut in half; squeeze out juice and seeds and chop pulp. Mix tomato, halibut, scallops and shrimp with remaining ingredients. Cover and chill at least 2 hours.

    Drain fish and serve with lime wedges. Serves eight.

CHILLED LUNCHEON HALIBUT

2-1/2 lbs. halibut fillets
Flour
1/3 cup olive oil
3 shallots, minced
1/2 cup white-wine vinegar
1/2 tsp. rosemary

❖

Dredge fillets with flour. Fry in oil until golden. Remove fish and pour excess oil from pan. Add remaining ingredients to pan and simmer, stirring. Arrange fillets in bottom of shallow glass dish and pour vinegar mixture over. Cover and refrigerate overnight. Serves six.

KEY LIME HALIBUT

3/4 lb. halibut fillet, cut into 1/2-inch cubes
1/2 cup key lime juice
1/4 tsp. salt
2 tsp. soy sauce
2 tsp. sugar
1 tbsp. onion, minced
1 lime

❖

Mix lime juice, salt, soy sauce and sugar and pour over fish. Cover and chill for at least six hours. Mix fish and onion. Squeeze on lime juice. Serves four.

HOT PICKLED HALIBUT

2 lbs. halibut fillets, cut into 1-inch cubes
4 medium-size potatoes, pared and diced
1 large onion, sliced
1 tbsp. sugar
2 tsp. salt
1/4 tsp. pepper
1 tbsp. Worcestershire sauce
1 tsp. mixed pickling spices, tied in cheesecloth
3 cans (about 1 lb. each) tomatoes
1 fresh lime
2 tbsp. butter

❖

Combine potatoes, onion, sugar, salt, pepper, Worcestershire sauce, pickling spices and tomatoes in large kettle. Bring to boil. Cover and reduce heat. Simmer about 30 minutes or just until potatoes are tender.

Add fish to potato mixture. Cover and cook 12 to 15 minutes. Remove spice bag. Put into serving tureen. Stir in juice from half the lime. Top with butter and garnish with the other half of lime, sliced. Serves eight.

HALIBUT IN A PICKLE

1 lb. halibut fillets, cut into small pieces
Flour for dredging
4 medium onions, sliced
1 cup white vinegar
1 tsp. turmeric
2 tsp. curry powder
1 tsp. peppercorns
2 bay leaves
2 tsp. brown sugar

❖

Dip halibut in flour to coat. Put onion slices in a baking dish and lay fish on top. Combine remaining ingredients and pour over fish and onions. Cover with a tight-fitting lid or seal with foil and bake for 1 hour. Remove from the oven and let cool. Refrigerate for 2 days before serving.

HALIBUT
COCKTAIL

1-1/2 cups cooked halibut, flaked
1/2 cup chili sauce
1 tbsp. prepared white horseradish
1 tbsp. fresh lemon juice
1 tsp. salt
1/8 tsp. pepper
4 lettuce leaves, shredded

❖

Chill halibut for several hours. Combine remaining ingredients, except lettuce, to make sauce. Chill. Arrange fish on lettuce in chilled cocktail glasses. Top with sauce. Serve very cold. Serves four.

SEAFOOD
NEWBURG

1-1/2 cups cooked halibut, cubed
1-1/2 cups cooked salmon cubed
4 tbsp. butter
3 tbsp. flour
2 cups light cream
1/4 cup sherry
2 egg yolks, beaten
Paprika
Salt

In 2-quart saucepan, combine butter, flour, and cream. Heat over medium heat, stirring constantly, until sauce is smooth and thick and is just beginning to simmer. Stir in sherry and eggs. Season to taste with paprika and salt. Stir in halibut and salmon cubes and heat over very low heat just until fish is warm. Serve on toast.

HALIBUT SANDWICH SPREAD

4 oz. cooked halibut, flaked
2 tsp. celery, finely chopped
1 tsp. onion, finely chopped
2 tsp. dill pickle, finely chopped
2 tbsp. mayonnaise
Salt and pepper to taste
1 tsp. cider vinegar
Dash of garlic powder

❖

Mix all ingredients well. Serve on bread or crackers. Serves two.

GRILLED HALIBUT SANDWICHES

2 cups smoked halibut, finely flaked
1 cup crushed pineapple, well drained
Mayonnaise
Bread slices

❖

Mix fish and pineapple and mayonnaise to produce a spread. Spread between bread slices buttered on the outer sides. Grill until the bread is well browned. Serves four.

HALIBUT BURGERS

2 cups cooked halibut, flaked
1/2 cup mayonnaise
1/2 tsp. salt
1/2 tsp. Worcestershire sauce
2 tbsp. onion, finely chopped
2 tsp. lemon juice
6 buttered, heated hamburger buns
Lettuce
6 slices tomato

❖

Combine all ingredients with fish except lettuce and tomato. Spread filling on heated buns. Add a leaf of lettuce and a slice of tomato. Makes six sandwiches.

HALIBUT SANDWICH

1 lb. halibut fillets, cut into four pieces
1 can Italian style stewed tomatoes, drained
4 slices bread, toasted
Cayenne

❖

Place halibut in a baking dish and bake in a pre-heated 350° oven for 10 minutes. Sprinkle cayenne lightly on top of the halibut and top with tomatoes. Bake for another five minutes. Serve over toast. Serves four.

SCANDINAVIAN HALIBUT PUDDING

1-1/2 lbs halibut fillet
4 tbsp. butter
1/4 cup cream
2 egg whites, beaten stiff
1/2 tsp. salt

❖

Mix halibut and butter in blender. Add salt and cream gradually. Blend well. Fold in egg whites. Turn into a buttered mold, filling 3/4 full. Set in a pan of hot water; cover and cook at 325° until set, usually one hour.

Unmold and serve. Serves four.

HALIBUT PUDDING

1-1/2 lbs. halibut
1-1/2 cups heavy cream
1 tbsp. cornstarch
Salt and white pepper
Fresh bread crumbs
Fresh dill sprigs

❖

Divide halibut into 2 or 3 parts and puree with cream, cornstarch and seasonings in a blender until smooth. Butter 6 individual molds and coat with bread crumbs. Fill molds almost to the top with halibut mixture and cover securely with foil.

Set in a baking pan and fill pan with enough water to come halfway up the sides of the molds. Bake at 325° F for about 45 minutes, or until puddings are firm. Don't let water boil. Add more heated water if needed. Serve with sauce of your choice. Garnish with fresh dill. Serves six.

HALIBUT TIMBALES

1/2 lb. halibut fillets
1 cup bread crumbs
1/2 cup milk
1 tsp. salt
A dash of white pepper
5 egg whites

Grind raw fish. Heat bread crumbs with milk. Stir to a smooth paste. Remove from heat and add fish, salt and pepper. Fold in stiffly beaten whites. Fill well-buttered individual molds. Set in a pan of hot water and bake at 350° for 20 minutes, until timbales are set and firm to the touch. Serve with tartar sauce or Hollandaise sauce. Serves four.

BROILED
HALIBUT CANAPES

1 cup cooked halibut, flaked
6 slices white bread
1/4 cup butter
1/3 cup chili sauce
1/4 lb. processed cheese, grated

✣

Toast bread on one side; trim off crusts and cut into rectangles. Butter untoasted side, cover with layer of halibut, then chili sauce, and top with cheese. Place canapes on baking sheet under broiler. Broil until cheese melts and canapes are heated. Makes 12 canapes.

HALIBUT DIP

1-1/2 cup cooked halibut, flaked
1/2 cup mayonnaise
1/4 cup stuffed olives, finely chopped
Salt, pepper and grated onion to taste
Crackers

❖

Combine all ingredients except crackers. Blend well and chill. Serve with crackers. Makes 1 pint.

CUCUMBER-HALIBUT APPETIZER

1/2 lb. fillet of halibut, chopped finely
1/4 cup shoyu
1/4 cup vinegar
2 tsp. sugar
1/4 tsp. ginger, freshly grated
3 medium cucumbers

❖

Combine shoyu, vinegar, sugar and ginger in a bowl. Stir in chopped halibut. Let mixture stand 1 hour. Peel cucumbers; cut in half lengthwise and scoop out the seeds. Slice very thin. Pour halibut mixture over sliced cucumbers and let stand 15 minutes. Serve with crackers.

BAKED HALIBUT APPETIZERS

1 lb. cooked halibut cut into small pieces
3 tbsp. butter
3 tbsp. flour
3/4 cup white wine
1/4 cup light cream
1 cup grated Cheddar cheese

Melt butter and blend in flour. Gradually add wine and cream. Stir until thick. Add half of the cheese and stir until melted. Add halibut. Spoon into six individual baking dishes and top with remaining cheese. Bake at 350° about 10 minutes. Serves six.

SMOKED HALIBUT AND CHEESE DIP

1-1/2 cups smoked halibut, flaked
6 oz. cream cheese
1 clove garlic, finely minced
3 tbsp. minced onion
1/4 tsp. salt
2 tbsp. Worcestershire sauce
1 tbsp. lemon juice
Strips of pimento

Mash halibut with cheese and blend in the seasonings. Chill several hours. Garnish with pimento strips. Serve with crackers or chips. Makes about 2-1/4 cups.

LAST-MINUTE HALIBUT DIP

1 cup cooked halibut, shredded
1 pint sour cream
1 package onion soup mix

❖

Mix all three ingredients. Serve with crackers, toast or chips.

DEEP-FRIED HALIBUT BALLS

3 lbs. halibut
4 cups potatoes, diced, unpeeled
2 cups water
1/4 tsp. ground pepper
2 tbsp. oil
2 tsp. maple syrup
Choice of herbs to taste (dillweed, parsley,
    marjoram, etc.)
4 cups oil for deep frying

❖

Boil fish, potatoes and water in a covered pot for 25 minutes. Drain and mash. Add the remaining ingredients and shape into 2-inch balls. Deep fry in hot oil until golden. Drain on paper and serve either hot or cold. Serves ten.

CIOPPINO

1 lb. halibut fillets, cut into 1-inch cubes
1/2 cup olive oil
2 large onions, finely chopped
2 large cloves garlic, finely chopped
1 can (2 lbs., 3 oz.) Italian plum tomatoes
1 can (6 oz.) tomato paste
1 cup dry red wine
2 tsp. leaf basil, crumbled
1 tsp. leaf oregano, crumbled
1 tsp. salt
1/2 tsp. freshly ground black pepper
2 dungeness crabs, cleaned and cracked
1 lb. shrimp, shelled and de-veined
18 littlenecks or cherrystone clams,
  well scrubbed
1/4 cup fresh parsley, chopped

❖

Saute onion in olive oil until tender but not browned. Add garlic and cook 2 minutes. Add tomatoes, tomato paste, wine, basil, oregano, salt and pepper. Bring to a boil and simmer 20 minutes. Add halibut, crabs, shrimp, and clams. Cover and simmer 10 minutes. Sprinkle with parsley. Serves six.

MEDITERRANEAN SEAFOOD CHOWDER

1 lb. halibut fillets, cut into 1-inch cubes
1 (4-1/2 oz.) can shrimp, drained
1 (7-1/2 oz.) can minced clams
1/4 cup green pepper, chopped
2 tbsp. onion, finely chopped
1 clove garlic, minced
1 tbsp. cooking oil
1 (16 oz.) can tomatoes, cut up
1 (8 oz.) can tomato sauce
1/2 cup dry red wine
3 tbsp. snipped parsley
1/4 tsp. salt
1/4 tsp. dried oregano, crushed
1/4 tsp. dried basil, crushed

❖

Saute green pepper, onion and garlic in oil till tender but not brown. Add undrained tomatoes, tomato sauce, wine, parsley, salt, oregano, basil, and dash pepper. Bring to boil. Reduce heat, cover and simmer 20 minutes.

Add halibut to broth. Simmer for 5 minutes. Add shrimp and undrained clams. Continue simmering, covered, about 3 minutes more. Serves six.

NEW ENGLAND
SMOKED HALIBUT CHOWDER

1/2 lb. smoked halibut, flaked
4 onions, sliced thinly
3 potatoes, cubed
1/2 tbsp. butter
1 tbsp. parsley, chopped
1 quart milk
1/4 tsp. pepper
Salt

❖

Cover onions with boiling water and simmer until half done. Add potatoes and enough boiling water to cover and cook for ten minutes. Add halibut and cook for another ten minutes. Add remaining ingredients and cook for five minutes. Serve with crackers. Serves eight.

MAIN COURSES

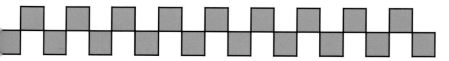

HALIBUT VINAIGRETTE

1-1/2 lb. halibut fillets, cut in four pieces
1/2 cup flour
5 tbsp. butter
1/4 cup fresh lemon juice
Peel of 1 lemon, grated (yellow part only)
1/2 tsp. salt
Dash of hot pepper sauce
1 clove garlic, minced
1/2 cup vegetable or corn oil
Sliced green onion
Carrot curls or grated carrots
Chopped fresh parsley
Black or green olives
Lemon wedges

❖

Dip fillets in flour. Saute them in butter, turning once. Carefully remove fillets to a serving platter. Mix lemon juice, peel, salt, pepper, hot pepper sauce, garlic and oil together and pour over fish. Refrigerate for at least 6 hours. Garnish with lemon wedges. Serves four.

HALIBUT LOAF

2 cups flaked halibut
1 chicken bouillon cube
3/4 cups boiling water
1-1/2 cups soft bread crumbs
1/2 cup chopped celery
1 tbsp. chopped parsley
1/2 cup light cream
1 tsp. grated onion
1 tsp. salt
Dash pepper
2 tsp. lemon juice
2 eggs beaten

❖

Dissolve bouillon cube in boiling water. Combine all ingredients. Place in a well greased 9-1/2 x 2-3/4 inch loaf pan. Bake at 350° for 1 hour or until loaf is firm in the center. Serves six.

HALIBUT SCRAPPLE

1/2 cup halibut, flaked and cooked
1 cup cornmeal
1 tbsp. flour
1 tsp. salt
1/4 tsp. pepper
1 cup cold water
3 cups boiling water

Mix cornmeal, flour, salt and pepper with 1 cup water. Boil 3 cups of water and slowly add to the cornmeal mixture which has been placed in a double boiler. Cover and cook at high steam for 2-1/2 hours, stirring frequently.

Add halibut and steam for another 30 minutes. Pour in a greased loaf pan and cover with waxed paper. Chill. Slice and fry in butter. Serves ten.

SMOKED HALIBUT SCRAMBLE

1/2 lb. smoked halibut
12 eggs
1/2 cup cream
4 tbsp. butter
Pepper

❖

Steam halibut over low heat for 15 minutes; break into small pieces. Beat eggs with cream and pepper to taste. Stir in halibut. Melt butter over low heat. Add eggs and halibut mixture and scramble. Serves six.

HALIBUT HASH

2 cups cooked halibut, flaked
4 potatoes
2 onions, coarsely chopped
4 tbsp. butter
Salt and pepper to taste

❖

Peel potatoes and let them boil in water to cover until just soft. Place them in cold water to keep them from cooking too much. Dice the potatoes. Saute onions over medium heat in oil until they are limp. Mix together fish, potatoes, and onion. Season to taste. Melt butter in skillet. Spread hash evenly over the pan and cook, gently until a good crust forms on the bottom. Serves four.

CURRIED HALIBUT BALLS

2 lbs. halibut fillets, chopped very fine
1/2 cup peanut oil
3 onions, minced
1/2 tsp. chili pepper, ground
4 garlic cloves, minced
1 tsp. lemon rind, grated
1 tsp. turmeric
2 tsps salt
1/4 cup flour
3 tomatoes, chopped

Saute onions, chile peppers, garlic, lemon rind, turmeric and salt for ten minutes in 1/4 cup of oil. Remove 1/3 of mixture and add halibut to it. Blend together until smooth. Form into walnut-sized balls and roll lightly in flour. Add oil to pan and heat. Add balls and brown on all sides. Add tomatoes and cook over low heat for 25 minutes. Serves six.

NEW ENGLAND HALIBUT BALLS

1 cup cooked halibut, flaked
1 egg, beaten
2 tsp. onion, grated
1 cup cracker or bread crumbs
1-1/2 cups mashed potatoes
1 tbsp. butter
1 tsp. dry mustard
Salt and pepper to taste

✛

Mix fish, potatoes and egg. Add remaining ingredients. Beat for 5 minutes until light and smooth. Shape into balls. Roll in cracker crumbs. Fry in deep fat until brown. Serves six.

SMOKED HALIBUT CAKES

1 lb. smoked halibut, flaked
1/2 cup onion, chopped
2 tbsp. oil
2 cups cold mashed potatoes
1/4 cup parsley, chopped
1 egg, beaten
Dash of pepper
1/2 cup dry breadcrumbs

❖

Cook onion in oil until tender. Combine all ingredients except crumbs, and shape mixture into cakes. Roll cakes in breadcrumbs. Fry in hot oil at moderate heat until one side is brown. Turn carefully and fry till the other side is brown. Remove from the pan and drain on absorbent paper. Serves six.

ENGLISH FISH AND CHIPS

2 to 2-1/2 lbs. halibut fillets
1 cup flour
1/2 tsp. paprika
1/4 tsp. salt
1/8 tsp. pepper
3/4 cup beer
Oil for deep-frying
Malt vinegar
Lemon wedges
French fried potatoes

Skin fillets and cut into slices 1/2 to 3/4 inch thick; then cut slices into chunks 3 by 5 inches. Make a batter by mixing dry ingredients and slowly stirring in the beer. Beat until smooth. Heat oil in a deep-fryer to 375°. Dip each piece of fish into batter, drain briefly. Deep-fry a few pieces at a time until golden brown. Drain. Serve with malt vinegar, salt, lemon wedges, and French fried potatoes. Serves four to six.

DEEP FRIED HALIBUT BITS

2 lbs. halibut fillets, cut into 1-inch cubes
1 egg, beaten
3/4 cups milk
1/4 tsp. pepper
1/2 tsp. salt
1 tsp. marjoram
1 tsp. baking powder
1 cup flour
Deep frying oil

❖

Sift flour, baking powder, marjoram, salt and pepper together. Mix with egg and milk to form a batter. Dip halibut cubes into batter and deep fry. Serves six.

MONTAGUE ISLAND
FISH AND CHIPS

2 lbs. halibut, cut into 1-inch cubes
1-1/2 cups flour
1 tbsp. baking powder
2 eggs
1 cup milk
1 tsp. salt

❖

Sift dry ingredients in one bowl. In another, beat eggs and add milk. Add liquid to flour mixture and stir until smooth. Dip fish in batter and deep fry in hot oil until outside is golden brown. Drain on absorbent paper. Serves six.

HALIBUT
IN BEER BATTER

3 lbs. halibut fillets
1 cup evaporated milk, undiluted
1 cup flat beer
1 tbsp. soy sauce
1 tbsp. white vinegar
1 tbsp. salad oil
1 tbsp. mayonnaise
2 cups flour, about
Salt and pepper
Peanut oil for frying

Mix milk, beer, soy sauce, vinegar, oil and mayonnaise. Add enough flour to make a medium-thick
batter. Salt and pepper to taste. Let batter sit for at
least 30 minutes before using.

Flour fillets, dip them into batter, and fry in peanut
oil over medium heat until golden. Turn once while
cooking. Sprinkle cooked fish with salt, and serve
immediately with lemon wedges. Serves six.

HALIBUT DEEP FRIED
AT HIGH TIDE

1 lb. halibut fillet, cut in 1-inch strips
1 cup milk
1 cup flour
4 egg whites
1/2 cup olive oil
Salt and pepper to taste
1/2 cup warm water
1 package dry yeast
Oil for frying
Parsley, chopped

❖

Soak fish in milk for several hours.

Combine flour, egg whites, olive oil, salt, pepper,
water, and yeast. Mix into a smooth paste. Allow to rest
2 hours in a warm, draft-free place.

Drain fish and rinse; dry on paper towels. Heat oil.
Dip fish fillets in batter and drop into hot oil. Fry until
golden. Sprinkle with chopped parsley and serve
immediately with lemon wedges. Serves four.

HALIBUT CROQUETTES IN COCONUT CREAM

2 lbs. halibut fillets
2 onions, sliced
1/2 tsp. dried ground chili pepper
3 garlic cloves, minced
1 tbsp. minced fresh gingerroot
2 tbsp. lemon juice
1 tbsp. cornstarch
2 tsp. salt
1 cup oil
1 cup coconut cream

❖

Grind the fillets fine with one of the onions, the chili, garlic and ginger. Blend in lemon juice, cornstarch and salt. Shape into small croquettes and chill, covered, for about 1 hour. Heat oil and saute remaining onion until browned. Remove onion from oil and brown croquettes. Remove croquettes and pour off all but 1 tbsp. oil. Blend in coconut cream, bring to a boil and return croquettes. Cook over low heat for 10 minutes. Garnish with browned onion rings. Serves six.

HALIBUT AND RICE CROQUETTES

2 cups cooked halibut, flaked
1 small onion, minced
1/4 cup butter
1/3 cup flour
1-1/4 tsp. salt
1/8 tsp. white pepper
1 cup tomato juice
1 tsp. each Worcestershire and
   prepared horseradish
1 cup cold cooked rice
3/4 cup crushed corn flakes
1 egg
2 tbsp. cold water
Oil for deep frying

❖

Cook onion in butter until yellow. Blend in flour, salt, and pepper. Add tomato juice slowly and cook until thickened, stirring constantly. Add Worcestershire, horseradish, fish, and rice. Mix well. Chill for several hours.

Shape into 8 croquettes. Roll in cereal and dip into beaten egg mixed with cold water. Roll in cereal again. Chill for 1 hour.

Fry in hot oil (370° to 375° on a frying thermometer). Serves four.

SIMPLE HALIBUT CROQUETTES

2 cups cooked halibut, flaked
1 cup grated cheese
2 eggs, well beaten
1 tsp. salt
2 tbsp. lemon juice
1/2 cup dry bread crumbs
2 tbsp. butter, melted

❖

Combine all ingredients except bread crumbs. Shape into 6 individual croquettes and roll in crumbs. Bake in a moderate oven, 350°, for 25 to 30 minutes, or until brown. Serve plain or with a sauce. Serves six.

SIMPLE HALIBUT LOAF

2 cups cooked halibut, flaked
1/2 tsp. salt
2 eggs, separated
1 cup cream of chicken soup

❖

Combine halibut, salt, and beaten egg yolks with soup. Beat egg whites and fold into the fish mixture. Pour into greased baking dish and bake at 350° for 20 to 30 minutes. Serves four.

HALIBUT CUTLETS

2 cups cooked halibut, flaked
1/4 cup butter
1/2 cup flour
2 cups milk
Salt and pepper
1/4 tsp. dried tarragon
1 tsp. lemon juice
1 bay leaf
1 tsp. Worcestershire sauce
1 cup fine bread crumbs

❖

Make a white sauce with butter, flour and milk. Add salt, pepper and seasonings to taste. Cook in top of a double boiler for 15 minutes. Remove bay leaf and add fish. Cool. Drop large spoonsful of mixture onto crumbs, coat well, and flatten into cutlets. Chill thoroughly. Bake at 425°. Serves four.

HALIBUT TURNOVER

1 cup cooked halibut, flaked
1 cup flour
1/4 tsp. salt
4 tbsp. butter
Pepper
Ground thyme
Dillweed
Parsley, chopped
1-1/2 cups cooked rice
1 (4 oz.) can mushroom pieces, drained
2 hard-cooked eggs, sliced
1 egg, beaten
Melted butter
Lemon juice

❖

Make a pastry of flour, salt, butter and about 2 tbsp. cold water. Chill for at least 2 hours.

Roll into a large oval 3/8 inch thick on a floured board. Put onto oiled and floured cookie sheet. Season fish with salt, pepper and herbs to taste.

On half of the oval alternate layers of rice, mushrooms, egg slices dotted with butter, and fish, ending with rice. Fold dough over, crimp edges, and brush with beaten egg. Make 2 or 3 vertical slashes for vents in top. Bake at 450° for about 15 minutes.

Serve with melted butter seasoned with lemon juice to taste. Serves four.

HALIBUT MOUSSE

1-1/2 lbs. halibut fillets
2 egg whites
2 cups heavy cream
3/4 tsp. salt
1/4 tsp. fresh. ground pepper
1/4 tsp. grated nutmeg
Dash of cayenne

❖

Blend fish at high speed until very finely shredded, then pound with wooden spoon or mallet. Put in bowl over cracked ice. Gradually beat in egg whites with a whisk. Stir in cream a little at a time, making sure it is thoroughly absorbed. Season and let stand over ice for 1 hour.

Stir mousse and pour into a buttered mold. Cover with waxed paper or buttered brown paper. Place mold in a pan with 1 inch of hot water. Bake at 350° for about 25 minutes, or until firm. Unmold and serve hot. Serves four.

HALIBUT CARROT SOUFFLE

1 cup halibut, cooked and flaked
3 tbsp. butter
3 tbsp. flour
1 tsp. salt
Dash of pepper
1 cup milk
1 tbsp. lemon juice
4 tbsp. finely grated raw carrot
1 tbsp. chopped parsley
3 eggs, separated

❖

Melt butter. Stir in flour, salt and pepper. gradually add milk Cook and stir until it has thickened. Remove from heat and add halibut, lemon juice, carrot and parsley. Beat egg whites until stiff. Beat yolks and add to the fish. Fold in egg whites. Turn mixture into an ungreased 1-1/2 quart casserole. Place dish in a shallow pan of boiling water. Bake at 350° for 45 minutes. Serve immediately. Serves four.

HALIBUT AND CHEESE SOUFFLE

1 cup cooked halibut, flaked
1 cup scalded milk
1 cup soft bread crumbs
1/2 cup grated American cheese
2 tbsp. chopped pimiento
1/2 tsp. salt
3 egg yolks, well beaten
3 egg whites, stiffly beaten
1 tbsp. lemon juice

❖

Combine milk and bread crumbs with grated cheese. Add halibut, lemon juice, pimiento, salt, and well-beaten egg yolks. Beat egg whites until stiff and fold into mixture. Turn into buttered casserole, set in a pan of water, and then bake in moderately hot oven, 325° for 40 minutes or until golden brown. Serves four.

ORIENTAL
BROILED HALIBUT

1-1/2 lbs. halibut fillets, cut into thin strips
1/2 cup soy sauce
2 tbsp. sherry
3 tbsp. sugar
1/2 tsp. ground ginger
1 garlic clove, mashed

❖

Combine soy sauce, sherry, sugar, ginger and garlic. Marinate fish strips in mixture for 30 minutes. Thread on skewers and broil. Serves six.

HALIBUT
KABOBS

1-1/2 lbs. halibut fillets, cut into 1-1/2 inch cubes
1/2 cup olive oil
1/4 cup vinegar
1/4 tsp. red-pepper flakes
Salt and pepper to taste
18 dried bay leaves
Boiling water, if needed
Lemon wedges for garnish

Rinse fish cubes. Drain on paper towels. Combine olive oil, vinegar, red-pepper flakes, salt and black pepper. Add fish cubes. Marinate in refrigerator 2 hours or longer.

Place bay leaves in small bowl and cover with boiling water. Let stand 5 minutes. Drain. Alternate halibut cubes with bay leaves on 6 metal skewers. Place on broiler rack 4 inches from heat. Cook, turning frequently, until fish cubes are tender and browned on all sides. Do not overcook. Serve with lemon wedges. Serves six.

ORIENTAL FISH KABOBS

2 pounds halibut fillets cut into 1-inch pieces
1/2 cup peanut or vegetable oil
2 tsp. grated orange rind
1/4 cup orange juice
2 tbsp. soy sauce
1 tbsp. dry sherry
1 tsp. grated gingerroot
1 tsp. salt
1/4 tsp. pepper
3 small navel oranges, peeled and each cut into 6 wedges
3 green onions, sliced into 2-inch pieces and each halved lengthwise

Combine oil, orange rind, juice, soy, sherry, ginger-root, salt and pepper in large bowl. Add fish, oranges and onions. Stir to mix. Cover and marinate 30 minutes at room temperature or 2 hours in refrigerator.

Drain fish mixture, reserving marinade. Thread fish, oranges and scallions alternately onto six 12-inch skewers. Brush with some of the marinade. Grill kabobs over hot coals about 8 minutes or until fish is cooked throughout, turning once and basting with marinade. Serves six.

JAPANESE SKEWERED HALIBUT

1-1/2 lbs. halibut fillets
2 tbsp. sherry
3 tbsp. sugar
1/2 tsp ginger, ground
1/2 cup soy sauce
1 garlic clove, mashed

❖

Slice halibut into thin strips. Combine ingredients. Marinate halibut slices for 30 minutes. Thread halibut on a skewer and broil under medium heat until fish flakes. Serves six.

BAKED HALIBUT
WITH COCONUT AND CASHEWS

1 lb. halibut fillets, finely chopped
1/3 cup vegetable oil
1 cup grated fresh coconut
1 large onion, finely chopped
2 cloves garlic, finely chopped
2 canned mild green chilis, chopped
1/2 tsp. salt
1 tsp. curry powder
2 tbsp. unsalted cashews, chopped
1 tbsp. lemon juice
2 eggs, lightly beaten

❖

Saute coconut in 1 tbsp. oil until lightly browned. Saute onion in remaining oil until tender but not browned. Add garlic, chilis, salt, and curry powder and cook, stirring, 2 minutes. Add coconut, nuts and halibut. Cook 2 minutes. Cool slightly. Mix lemon juice with eggs and add to skillet. Divide halibut mixture among 6 oiled 7-inch squares of aluminum foil. Wrap tightly and place on a baking sheet. Bake at 375° for 20 minutes. Serves six.

SPICY HALIBUT CURRY

1 lb. halibut fillets, cut into 1-inch cubes
1/2 cup vegetable oil
1 large onion, finely chopped
1 clove garlic, finely chopped
1/4 tsp. turmeric
1/2 tsp. ground ginger
1/2 tsp. ground cumin
1/2 tsp. chili powder
1 large tomato, peeled, seeded, and chopped
1 container (8 ozs.) plain yogurt
1/2 tsp. salt
Parsley for garnish
Hot cooked rice to serve four

❖

Heat oil in a large heavy skillet and fry fish until browned and cooked. Remove fish to paper towels to drain.

Remove all but 2 tbsp. oil from skillet and saute the onion until tender but not browned. Add garlic, turmeric, ginger, cumin, and chili powder and cook, stirring, 2 minutes. Add tomato and cook 1 minute. Stir in yogurt and salt. Reheat but do not boil. Return fish and reheat but do not boil. Serve sprinkled with chopped parsley over hot cooked rice. Serves four.

CURRIED
HALIBUT

2 lbs. halibut
Salt
Juice of 1/2 lemon
3/4 cup oil
2 cups shredded fresh coconut
8 tsp. curry powder
8 tsp. ground cuminseed
4 tsp. chile powder
4 green chiles, seeded and ground
1/2 tsp. mashed garlic
3 tomatoes, peeled, seeded and chopped
1 green chile, halved and seeded
1 tsp. minced fresh coriander leaves
3/4 cup water
2 tsp. potato flour mixed with a little water
Lemon juice

❖

Rub halibut with salt. Add lemon juice. Heat oil and saute coconut in it until brown. Add curry powder, cumin seed, chili powder, ground green chiles and mashed garlic. Saute until brown. Add tomatoes, halved green chili, coriander leaves and water. Simmer for 5 minutes to blend flavors. Add flour mixture to sauce. Add fish to sauce; season with salt and more lemon juice to taste. Let sauce boil until fish is tender. Serves six.

POACHED HALIBUT WITH BUTTERMILK

3 lbs halibut fillets
1/2 tbsp. turmeric
6 cups buttermilk
1 tbsp. lemon juice
1 tsp. salt
1 tbsp. ground cuminseed
3 tbsp. green pepper, chopped
5 tbsp. butter
fresh ground pepper

❖

Rub halibut with turmeric and black papper. Poach in buttermilk 5 minutes. Remove halibut but keep it warm. To the liquid, add lemon juice and salt and simmer until the liquid is reduced by half. Add cumin seed, green peppers and warm halibut. Simmer for 10 minutes. Brown butter and add to the simmering halibut. Serves six.

HALIBUT
IN COCONUT CURRY

4 lbs. halibut fillets
1/2 cup oil
2 cups red onion, thinly sliced
2 tsp. ground ginger
1/4 cup ground cashews
1/2 tsp. dried ground chili pepper
1/4 tsp. ground saffron
2 cups coconut milk
3 tbsp. lime or lemon juice
1 tsp. sugar
1 tbsp. cornstarch
Salt

❖

Salt fillets and brown in 3 tbsp. oil. Remove from heat. Heat remainder of oil and saute onion slices until soft but not browned. Remove half of onions. Add to the pan ginger, cashews, chili pepper, saffron and coconut milk. Boil and add lime juice. Mix sugar and cornstarch together and add to sauce.

Return fillets to sauce and cook over low heat for 10 minutes. Serve with onions. Serves eight.

MUCHLI MOOLU

2 lbs. halibut, cut into 1-inch cubes
1/4 cup peanut oil
1/4 cup onion slices
1/2 cup onion slices, ground to a paste
1 tbsp. ground garlic
1/2 tsp. ground turmeric
3 cups coconut milk
1 tsp. salt
4 whole hot green chilis

✜

Heat oil in pan and fry fish cubes for 2 minutes. Remove fish and set aside.

Pour off half of the oil. Fry sliced onions in oil until light brown. Add onion paste, garlic paste and turmeric. Stir-fry for 2 minutes. Add coconut milk and bring to a boil, stirring frequently. Add salt, chilis and fish cubes. Continue to cook and baste for 10 minutes to reduce sauce to one-fourth of the original volume. Serve warm with rice. Serves six.

FISH MOLEE

1-1/2 lbs. halibut fillets
2 oz. butter
1 tbsp. onions, finely chopped
1/2 tsp. garlic, finely chopped
1/2 dozen fresh green chilis, cut lengthwise
　in halves
6 thin slices fresh or pickled green ginger
1/2 tsp. of ground turmeric
Thick coconut milk
Salt
4 cardamoms
4 cloves
A 2-inch stick of cinnamon

❖

Saute onions, garlic, spices and sliced ginger in butter. Cook, but do not brown the onions. Add turmeric and green chilis, stir and simmer for 2 or 3 minutes. Add coconut milk and salt to taste and gradually bring to boiling point. Add the fillets, but *do not* stir. Simmer until halibut is done. Serves four.

HAWAIIAN HALIBUT
WITH COCONUT MILK

1-1/2 lbs. halibut fillets
1/2 tsp. salt
4 tbsp. butter
3/4 cup coconut milk

❖

Sprinkle fish with salt and saute in butter until barely done. Add the coconut milk. Bring to a boil and simmer for 2 minutes. Serves four.

HALIBUT
HAWAII

3 lbs. halibut fillets
1/3 cup scallions, chopped with tops
2 tbsp. white sesame seeds, toasted and ground
1 tbsp. sesame oil
Dash of pepper
3 tbsp. soy sauce
1-1/2 tbsp. butter

❖

Mix scallions, sesame seeds, 1 tbsp. oil, pepper and soy sauce. Dip halibut into this mixture. Saute in butter until lightly browned. Serves six.

HALIBUT STEAKS HAWAIIAN

2 halibut steaks
1 cup cooked rice
1 cup bread cubes
2 tbsp. lemon juice
1 cup crushed pineapple, drained
3 tbsp. butter, melted
3 slices bacon
1/2 cup pineapple juice

❖

Combine rice, bread cubes, lemon juice, pineapple and salt. Place one steak in a well-greased baking pan; cover with rice mixture and place remaining steak over top. Brush with melted butter. Arrange bacon on top and pour pineapple juice around halibut. Bake at 350° until fish flakes. Serves two.

HALIBUT FILLETS HAWAIIAN

1 lb. halibut fillets
Flour
4 tbsp. butter
1/2 tsp. ground ginger
2 tbsp. brown sugar
2 tbsp. lemon juice
1/2 cup sherry
2 bananas

❖

Dip fillets into flour and saute in butter in a skillet until golden. Turn only once. Remove and keep warm.

Mix ginger, brown sugar, lemon juice in skillet and simmer for a few minutes. Add a little more butter if mixture is getting dry. Add bananas, cut lengthwise into halves, and cook for 2 minutes on each side. Serve halibut with sauce and bananas. Serves two.

HALIBUT ROAST HAWAIIAN

3 to 4 lb. halibut roast
Salt and pepper
3 strips bacon
1 (13-1/4 oz.) can pineapple tidbits
1-1/2 tbsp. cornstarch
3 tbsp. sugar
1/3 cup vinegar
1-1/2 tbsp. soy sauce
1/2 green pepper, cut into 3/4-inch cubes

❖

Season halibut with salt and pepper. Place bacon strips over top . Bake in 375° oven 45 minutes or until halibut flakes when tested with a fork.

Drain pineapple. Add water to syrup to make 1 cup. Combine cornstarch, sugar, vinegar, soy sauce and pineapple syrup. Cook, stirring constantly, until thick and clear. Add pineapple tidbits and green pepper. Heat through. Serve halibut with hot pineapple sauce. Serves 6 to 8.

MACADAMIA HALIBUT BITS

2 lbs. halibut fillets
2 cups oil
1/2 cup butter
1 small onion, halved
1 clove garlic, halved
1 cup flour
3 eggs
2 tbsp. soy sauce
1-1/2 cups yellow cornmeal
1 jar (3-1/2 oz.) Macadamia nuts, chopped

❖

In a deep saucepan combine oil, butter, onion and garlic. Heat oil to 350°. Remove onion and garlic when golden brown. Cut halibut into portions about 3 x 3 inches. Dredge each portion in flour, shaking off excess. Beat together eggs and soy sauce. Dip each fillet into egg mixture. Combine cornmeal and Macadamia nuts. Dip each fillet into this mixture and press coating lightly. Fry fillets 3-1/2 to 4 minutes. Makes 4 to 6 servings.

HALIBUT AND MACADAMIA NUTS

4 halibut fillets
1/2 stick melted butter
1/4 cup Parmesan cheese
1/2 cup Macadamia nuts, chopped

Coat halibut with melted butter. Sprinkle with Parmesan cheese and chopped Macadamia nuts. Spoon butter over fish. Bake at 400° for 20 minutes, or until halibut flakes. Serves four.

HALIBUT STIR-FRY

1 lb. halibut fillets, cut into 1/2-inch wide strips
4 tbsp. soy sauce
1 tsp. minced ginger root or ground ginger
6 tbsp. corn oil
1/2 lb. fresh bean sprouts
1 cup sliced celery
3 green onions, cut in sections (include tops)
2 tbsp. cornstarch
1 tsp. sugar
1/2 cup water
1 cup shredded red cabbage
1 lb. fresh, washed, crisped spinach
3 cups hot, cooked rice

❖

Marinate fish in soy sauce and ginger for 15 minutes. Heat oil in a skillet. Remove fish from marinade; save the marinade. Brown fish on both sides in skillet, turning it carefully. Remove fish to a serving platter.

Saute bean sprouts, celery, and onions in the skillet for 2 to 4 minutes. Combine cornstarch, sugar, and water. Add, with the marinade, to vegetables. Mix well, stirring until thickened. Add red cabbage and spinach and stir-fry quickly until the spinach begins to wilt or go limp. Return fish to the skillet. Gently stir all ingredients. Serve with hot, cooked rice. Serves six.

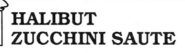

HALIBUT
ZUCCHINI SAUTE

1/2 to 3/4 lb. halibut steaks
Salt and pepper
1 small zucchini, sliced
1/4 cup onion, coarsely chopped
1 clove garlic, minced
3 tbsp. oil
1 medium tomato, cut into wedges
1 tbsp. chopped parsley
1 tbsp. lemon juice

❖

Sprinkle halibut with salt and pepper. Saute zucchini, onion and garlic in 1 tbsp. oil for 2 minutes. Add tomato and parsley. Cook, covered, 1 minute. Remove from pan.

Saute halibut in 2 tbsp. hot oil until brown on both sides. Cook until halibut flakes easily when tested with a fork. Return vegetables to pan. Add lemon juice; salt and pepper to taste. Serves two.

HALIBUT
SAUTE

1 lb. halibut, cut into 1-inch cubes
Salt and pepper
3 tbsp. oil
1 cup each thinly sliced carrots, sliced celery,
   diagonally sliced green onion and broccoli
   flowerets
1/4 tsp. grated gingerroot
1/4 cup chickenstock
2 tsp. cornstarch
1 tsp. grated lemon or lime peel

❖

    Season halibut with salt and pepper. Saute in 2
tbsp. oil until barely cooked; remove halibut from
skillet. Saute vegetables in remaining oil until tender.
Return halibut to skillet. Add 1/4 tsp. salt and ginger.
Combine chicken stock, cornstarch and lemon peel.
Add to fish mixture. Cook and stir until thickened and
halibut flakes easily when tested with a fork. Serves
four.

HALIBUT
AND CUCUMBER SAUTE

2 lbs. halibut fillets, cut into 3-inch wide strips
2 small cucumbers
3 tbsp. butter
1/4 cup onion, finely chopped
Salt and pepper to taste
Flour seasoned with salt and pepper
4 tbsp. vegetable oil
1 cup dry white wine
Lemon juice
1 tbsp. parsley, finely chopped

❖

Peel cucumbers. Cut in half and remove seeds. Cut into cubes 1/2-inch square. Melt butter in a small skillet. Add onion and saute 1 minute. Add cucumber cubes, salt, and pepper. Saute 5 minutes, stirring occasionally. Set aside.

Flour fish lightly, shaking off excess. Place in a skillet containing hot vegetable oil. Quickly fry fish over moderately high heat, about 1 minute to a side, removing each piece as it finishes cooking. When all the fish is done, pour off any excess oil from the pan. Pour in wine and stir constantly until it begins to thicken. Add fish and cucumber and onion mixture to skillet and mix gently until all is coated with sauce. Season with salt, pepper, and lemon juice to taste. Stir in parsley and allow to cook until fish is heated through. Serve immediately. Serves four.

HALIBUT PIE
WITH RUTABAGA SAUCE

1 lb. halibut fillet
1 lb. potato, cooked
2-3/4 cup milk
1 cup frozen peas
4 tbsp. butter
3 tbsp. all-purpose flour
1 cup Cheddar cheese, grated
1 large rutabaga
1/2 tsp. grated nutmeg
1 tbsp. parsley, chopped

❖

Mash potato; flavor with salt and pepper if desired. Add enough milk (1/4 cup) to give consistency for forcing through a pastry bag. Keep hot. Poach fish in 2-1/2 cups milk. Remove fish and flake.

Melt 2 tbsp. butter in a saucepan and stir in flour. Cook 1 minute, stirring. Gradually add strained milk from cooking the fish and bring to boil, stirring constantly, until sauce is smooth and thickened. Add peas and grated cheese and reheat until bubbling. Lightly fold in flaked fish and pour into a warm baking dish. Place the warm potatoes in a pastry bag fitted with a large star nozzle. Make large potato rosettes on the fish mixture. Place under a moderately hot grill for a few minutes until the surface turns golden brown.

Peel, chop, and cook rutabaga until tender in boiling salted water. Drain well and mash with 2 tbsp. butter, nutmeg, salt, and pepper. Turn puree into a warm serving dish. Dot with butter and sprinkle with parsley. Serves four.

HALIBUT FLORENTINE

2 lbs. halibut
2 (10 oz.) packages frozen chopped spinach,
   cooked and well drained.
1/2 lb. sharp cheddar cheese, grated
1/4 cup slivered almonds, toasted
3 tbsp. butter or margarine
3 tbsp. flour
3 cups milk
1 tbsp. lemon juice
1 tsp. dry mustard
1 tsp. Worcestershire sauce
1/2 tsp. salt
1/8 tsp. black pepper
1/8 tsp. nutmeg
1 (8 oz.) package medium egg noodles

❖

Melt butter over medium heat. Stir in flour and slowly add milk, about a 1/4 cup at a time, stirring constantly until it thickens and comes to a boil. Add lemon juice, mustard, Worcestershire sauce, salt, pepper, nutmeg, and 1 cup of cheese. Stir until melted completely. Cook egg noodles and drain.

Pour half cheese sauce over noodles and stir together. Put this into a large casserole. Arrange spinach over noodles. Arrange fish over spinach. Cover with remaining sauce. Sprinkle reserved cheese and almonds on top. Bake in a preheated 375° oven for about 30 minutes. Serves six.

HALIBUT STUFFED WITH CRABMEAT

2-1/2 halibut fillets, 8 pieces
1/4 cup onion,chopped
1/4 cup butter
1 (3 oz.) can mushrooms, drained; save juice
1 (7-1/2 oz.) can crabmeat
1/2 cup saltine cracker crumbs
2 tbsp. parsley
1/2 tsp. salt
3 tbsp. butter
3 tbsp. flour
1/4 tsp. salt
Milk
1/3 cup dry white wine
4 oz. (1 cup) Swiss cheese, shredded
1/2 tsp. paprika

❖

Saute onion and butter until tender. Stir in drained mushrooms, crabmeat, cracker crumbs, parsley, salt and dash of pepper. Spread mixture on fillets. Bring both ends up and overlap. Put in 12 x 7-1/2 x 2-inch baking dish seam side down.

In saucepan, melt butter. Blend in flour and salt. Add enough milk to mushroom juice to make 1-1/2 cups. Add wine and cook until thickened. Pour over fillets. Bake 25 minutes at 400°.

Sprinkle cheese and paprika over fillets and return to oven for 10 more minutes. Serves six.

HALIBUT ROLL-UPS
WITH BLUE CHEESE STUFFING

2 lbs. halibut fillets
1/2 cup butter
1/4 cup minced fresh parsley
1 medium fresh tomato, chopped
1/2 cup minced celery
1/4 cup firmly packed blue cheese
3 cups soft bread crumbs
1 egg well beaten
1/2 tsp. salt
Juice of 1 lemon

❖

Melt 1/4 butter in skillet. Add parsley, tomato and celery. Cook, stirring often, for 10 minutes. Remove from heat. Crumble cheese into mixture. Add crumbs, egg and salt. Mix well. Spread mixture on fillets; roll up, fasten with toothpicks.

Butter an oblong 1-1/2-quart baking dish. Melt remaining 1/4 cup of butter; mix with juice of 1 lemon. Pour over fish rolls. Bake in 350° oven until fish flakes easily. Serves six.

SAUTEED HALIBUT WITH GINGER

1-1/2 lb. halibut fillets
1/2 tsp. salt
White pepper to taste
1/2 cup all-purpose flour
1 stick (1/4 lb.) butter
1 tbsp. freshly grated ginger
4 scallions, finely chopped
3 tbsp. lemon juice

❖

Mix salt, pepper, and flour in a shallow pan. Dip fillets in flour and shaking off excess flour. Melt butter in large frying pan over medium high heat Saute fillets 2 minutes on each side. Remove and keep warm.

Stir ginger, scallions, and lemon juice in remaining butter and pour over fish. Serves four.

BOILED HALIBUT
WITH HORSERADISH SAUCE

4 pounds halibut fillet
1-1/2 tsp. salt
1 cup white wine
2 cups water
1/2 onion, minced
1/4 lb. mushrooms, chopped
1/4 tsp. pepper
2 tbsp. chopped parsley
3 tbsp. grated fresh horseradish
1 cup sour cream

✛

Cut halibut in serving-size pieces. Rub salt lightly on fillet. Place in saucepan. Add wine, water, onion, mushrooms, pepper, and parsley. Bring to a boil. Cover; lower heat and cook gently 20 minutes, or until halibut flakes. Remove and keep warm.

Cook pan juices rapidly to reduce them. Pour over fish. Mix horseradish and cream; serve with fish. Serves six.

HALIBUT FILLETS WITH WINE

1-1/2 lbs. halibut fillets
Salt and pepper to taste
1/2 cup dry white wine
1/2 cup boiling water
1 sweet red pepper, diced
1 cup medium white sauce
2 tbsp. buttered crumbs
2 tbsp. grated cheese

❖

Skewer fillets in rolls and place in buttered baking dish. Season. Mix wine and water and pour over the halibut. Cover and bake at 400° for 25 minutes.

Mix red pepper with white sauce and pour over the halibut. Sprinkle with crumbs and cheese and brown under broiler. Serves four.

POACHED HALIBUT
WITH BUTTER SAUCE

1 lb. halibut fillets
1 thick slice each onion and lime
1/2 tsp. salt
1 small bay leaf
4 peppercorns
Water
2 tbsp. butter, softened
1-1/2 tsp. parsley, minced
1-1/2 tsp. lime juice
1 tsp. lime peel, grated

✜

Combine onion, lime, salt, bay leaf, halibut and peppercorns. Add just enough water to cover; bring to boil. Reduce heat and simmer, covered, until halibut flakes. Transfer the halibut to serving platter and keep warm.

Combine butter, parsley, lime juice and lime peel. Blend thoroughly. Makes about 3 tablespoons. Spread on halibut. Serves two.

FILLET OF HALIBUT WITH LOBSTER SAUCE

1 lb. halibut fillets
1 shallot, chopped
1 tsp. salt
1/4 tsp. white pepper
1/4 cup white wine
1/4 cup bouillon
2 tbsp. butter
2 tbsp. flour
1 egg yolk
1/4 cup cream
1/4 cup butter
1 tsp. lobster paste
1/4 tsp. onion juice
1/4 tsp. lemon juice

Place halibut and shallot in saucepan. Season with salt and pepper. Add wine and bouillon. Cook uncovered until fish is tender and liquid is reduced to about half the original amount. Remove fish to broiling pan and keep warm. Beat butter and flour together; stir into pan liquid and cook until slightly thickened. Beat egg and cream together; stir into sauce. Heat a moment, but do not boil.

Let butter soften to room temperature. Beat lobster paste, lemon juice and onion juice into it until smooth. Makes about 1/4 cup.

Spread lobster butter over halibut and pour hot sauce over it. Set under broiler for 2 or 3 minutes. Serves four.

HALIBUT
WITH NUT SAUCE

2 lb. halibut roast
Salt
1/4 cup olive oil
1 garlic clove
1/4 cup pine nuts or blanched almonds
1/4 cup parsley, minced
2 large onions, chopped
1 (1 lb.) can tomatoes
Pepper
1/2 tsp. sugar

❖

Sprinkle both sides of fish with salt and put in a shallow baking dish. Saute almonds and garlic in oil until golden. Remove garlic and nuts from oil and crush them into a paste, gradually adding parsley with a bit of oil from skillet. Add tomatoes to onions and simmer for 5 minutes. Stir in nut paste. Season with salt and pepper. Add sugar and pour over fish, covering it completely. Bake at 350° for 30 minutes. Serves six.

POACHED HALIBUT WITH SHRIMP SAUCE

2 lbs. halibut fillets
1 cup each dry white wine and water
1 tsp. salt
1 bay leaf
Dash thyme
2 tbsp. butter
2 tbsp. flour
2 egg yolks
1 tbsp. lemon juice
1 tbsp. parsley, minced
1/2 lb. shrimp

❖

Place halibut in skillet with wine, water and seasonings. Bring to boil. Reduce heat and simmer, covered, until halibut flakes. Remove halibut and keep warm.

Strain poaching liquid and reserve. Melt butter and add flour; stir until smooth. Slowly add fish stock. Cook and stir until thickened. Combine egg yolks, lemon juice and parsley. Slowly stir into sauce. Add shrimp; simmer five minutes. Spoon sauce over the halibut. Serves six.

HALIBUT
WITH PINK PRAWN SAUCE

1-1/2 lbs. halibut fillets
1 lemon
Salt and ground black pepper
2 tbsp. butter
1/4 cup all-purpose flour
1-1/4 cup milk
1 tsp. salt
Black pepper to taste
2 tsp. tomato paste
2 tsp. paprika
2 (7 oz.) cans prawns

❖

Put fillets in baking dish. Spoon grated rind and juice of lemon over fillets and sprinkle with salt and pepper. Cover and bake at 350° for 20 minutes. Remove fillets and keep warm. Melt butter in saucepan, stir in the flour and cook for 1 minute.

Gradually add milk, seasoning, tomato paste, and paprika. Bring to boil, stirring constantly. Add any juices left from cooking the fish. Cook gently for 2 minutes. Meanwhile pound the prawns until smooth, and stir into the sauce. Season to taste. Serves four.

BROILED HALIBUT WITH RHUBARB AND TOMATO SAUCE

2 lbs. halibut fillets
2 tbsp. butter
3 tbsp. onion, finely chopped
3/4 lb. rhubarb, trimmed and cut
   into 3/4-inch slices
1 medium to large tomato, skinned, seeded
   and cubed
1 tbsp. sugar
Salt to taste
Pepper to taste
2 tbsp. vegetable oil
1/4 tsp. dried thyme

❖

    Saute onion in butter until it is translucent. Add rhubarb, tomato, sugar, salt, and pepper. Cover saucepan. Lower heat and cook for 6 minutes, stirring occasionally.

    Preheat broiler. Pour half the oil in the broiler pan and lay halibut fillets in the oil. Sprinkle rest of the oil over the halibut with a little salt, pepper, and thyme. Broil until cooked through and lightly browned on top, about 5 minutes. Serve rhubarb and tomato sauce alongside broiled fillets. Serves six.

BROILED HALIBUT WITH MUSHROOMS AND SOUR CREAM

2 lbs. halibut fillets
Juice of 2 limes
Salt and pepper to taste
3 tbsp. butter
1 cup sliced mushrooms
2 green onions, sliced
1 cup sour cream

❖

Place halibut in a shallow dish. Squeeze on lime juice. Season with salt and pepper, and let fish marinate for one hour, turning occasionally.

Place halibut on hot oiled broiler pan. Dot fish with 1 tbsp. of the butter. Cook 3 inches under broiler for 10-15 minutes, until it barely flakes. Don't turn. Baste while cooking.

Saute mushrooms and onions in remaining 2 tbsp. of butter until tender. When fish is almost cooked, heat sour cream in mushroom and onions. Serve halibut with sauce. Serves four.

BROILED HALIBUT
IN CLAM SAUCE

2 lbs. halibut fillet
2 tbsp. butter
2 tbsp. flour
1 can minced clams, drained with juice reserved
1/2 cup or more hot milk
Juice of 1/2 lemon plus 2 tbsp.
1/3 cup green onion, minced
1/4 cup green olives, sliced
1 tsp. prepared mustard
1/4 cup mayonnaise
Salt and pepper to taste

In a saucepan, heat butter and flour. Add clam juice from drained clams plus enough hot milk to make one cup. Cook, beating with a whisk, until sauce is smooth and boils. Stir in 2 tbsp. lemon juice, onion, olives, drained clams, mustard, mayonnaise, and 1/2 tsp. each of salt and pepper.

Preheat the broiler. Place halibut on a greased baking dish, season with salt and pepper, and the remaining lemon juice. Dot with butter, and broil for 5 or 6 minutes. Remove pan from broiler, turn fish over, and cover with clam sauce. Return dish to broiler and cook until fish is done and sauce is bubbly, about 5 minutes. Serves four.

BAKED HALIBUT
WITH ALMOND DRESSING

6 lbs. halibut fillets
1/2 cup lime juice
1/2 tsp. salt
1/4 tsp. fresh ground pepper
1/2 cup olive oil
1 large onion, thinly sliced
1/2 tsp. dried thyme
1/2 tsp. oregano
1 bay leaf, crumbled
1 medium onion, minced
2 garlic cloves, minced
1 fresh hot pepper, seeded and minced
1 tbsp. parsley, chopped
1/2 cup ground toasted almonds
1-1/2 cups water

❖

Mix lime juice with salt and pepper and pour over halibut to marinate. Pour 6 tbsp. olive oil into a baking dish. Arrange sliced onion in dish. Sprinkle with thyme, oregano, bay leaf, salt and pepper. Saute minced onion and garlic in remaining olive oil until tender. Add hot pepper, parsley, almonds and 1/2 cup water. Mix well.

Remove halibut and pour marinade over onions in the baking dish with remaining one cup water. Place halibut in dish. Spread almond dressing on top and sides of fish. Bake uncovered at 400° for 40-45 minutes or until halibut flakes. Serves six.

BAKED HALIBUT WITH CAPERS AND GREEN OLIVES

6 halibut fillets
1 tsp. garlic, minced
1/4 cup fresh lime juice
1/2 cup water
3/4 cup onions, sliced
12 pitted green olives, sliced
1/2 tsp. salt
1/2 tsp. pepper
1/2 cup olive oil
2 bay leaves, crushed
1 tbsp. each of capers and caper liquid

❖

Place halibut fillets on a lightly oiled baking dish. Blend remaining ingredients and smooth mixture over fish. Bake for 10 minutes at 450°, then reduce to 325° for 10 minutes. Serves six.

HALIBUT
WITH ORANGE SAUCE

1-1/2 pounds halibut steaks
1/2 cup orange juice
2 green onions, diagonally sliced
1 tbsp. lime or lemon juice
3 tbsp. oil, divided
1/4 tsp. ground ginger
1/8 tsp. salt
Seasoned flour
Orange slices

❖

Place halibut steaks in shallow baking dish. Combine orange juice, green onions, lime juice, 1 tbsp. oil, ginger and salt. Pour over halibut; marinate 30 minutes.

Dip halibut in seasoned flour. Saute in 2 tbsp. oil until halibut flakes. Turn steaks halfway through cooking time. Remove halibut and keep warm. Add marinade to the skillet and reduce to half the volume (about 1/3 cup). Pour over halibut. Garnish with orange slices. Serves four.

HALIBUT
WITH ANCHOVIES

2 halibut steaks
3 tbsp. olive oil
1 small onion, finely chopped
2 flat anchovy fillets
2 tbsp. parsley, chopped
Freshly ground pepper to taste
Flour for dredging

❖

Saute onion in butter until tender. Add anchovies and parsley and saute, mashing anchovies until they have mixed thoroughly with the onions. Season with pepper. Dredge steaks lightly with flour. Shake to remove excess. Heat remaining oil in a separate frying pan and fry steaks until golden on both sides. Remove steaks from pan and place on a heated serving dish. Pour anchovy-onion mixture over the top and serve. Serves two.

HALIBUT
WITH BANANA

1-1/2 lbs. halibut fillets
1 egg, slightly beaten
1/4 tsp. salt
1/8 tsp. pepper
1/4 tsp. garlic salt
1/2 cup fine dry bread crumbs
5 to 6 tbsp. butter or margarine
3 firm green-tipped bananas, cut lengthwise
Lemon wedges

❖

Dip fillets in beaten egg. Mix salt, pepper, garlic salt, and crumbs in a bag and shake fillets one at a time in the mixture. Melt 3 tbsp. butter in a large frying pan over medium heat. Fry fillets until brown on both sides and easily flakes. Remove halibut to a warm platter; quickly brown bananas on all sides and arrange on platter with fish. Garnish with lemon. Serves four.

GRILLED FISH
WITH OLIVE SAUCE

2 lbs. halibut steaks
1 tsp. pepper
1/4 cup olive oil
1/2 cup pitted black olives, coarsely chopped
2 tsp. lemon juice
1 tsp. garlic, finely chopped

Press pepper into steaks and brush with oil. Grill over moderately hot coals, turning once until fish flakes when pierced with a fork.

Meanwhile, combine olives, lemon juice and garlic in a small bowl; stir to mix well. Place halibut on a platter and top with olive mixture. Serves four.

BAKED HALIBUT
WITH MUSHROOMS

2 lbs. halibut fillets
1 tsp. salt
2 tbsp. butter
1 can mushrooms, drained
I cup sour cream
1/4 cup sherry wine
Paprika

❖

Place halibut in buttered baking dish. Season and bake at 425° for ten minutes. Saute mushrooms in butter and remove from heat. Add wine and cream and heat. Pour over halibut. Continue to bake at 375° until fish flakes. Sprinkle with paprika. Serves six.

HALIBUT STEAKS
WITH MUSHROOM SAUCE

2 lbs. halibut steaks, 1 inch thick
1/2 lb. mushrooms, thinly sliced
3 tbsp. butter
2 small tomatoes, peeled, seeded and chopped
1 garlic clove, minced
Salt and pepper

❖

Saute mushrooms in butter until tender. Add tomatoes and garlic. Heat through and season to taste. Place halibut in a buttered baking dish. Sprinkle with salt and pepper and spoon mushroom sauce on top. Bake, uncovered, at 400° for 25 to 30 minutes or until steaks flake. Serves six.

HALIBUT STEAKS
WITH VEGETABLES

6 halibut steaks
1 medium-size onion, minced
1 bunch of scallions, chopped
1/4 cup olive oil
4 celery ribs, minced
3 carrots, sliced
1 lb. spinach, chopped
1/2 cup parsley, minced
1 cup canned tomatoes
5 mint leaves, chopped
2 garlic cloves, minced
Salt and pepper to taste

Saute onion and scallions in oil until tender. Add celery, carrots, spinach, parsley, tomatoes, mint, garlic, salt, and pepper. Simmer for 15 minutes. Spoon half of the vegetable mixture into a buttered baking dish. Cover with steaks and spoon on rest of mixture. Cover and bake at 325° for one hour. Serves six.

HALIBUT
WITH CREAMY MUSTARD SAUCE

4 halibut steaks
1/4 cup butter, melted
1/4 cup flour
1/2 tsp. dry mustard
1/2 tsp. steak sauce
3/4 tsp. salt
Dash of pepper
2 cups milk
1 tbsp. chives, minced
Paprika

❖

Poach halibut in simmering water to cover until fish flakes. Drain and leave halibut in covered pan. Blend butter, flour and seasonings. Add milk and cook until thickened. Pour sauce over halibut. Sprinkle with chives and paprika. Serves four.

FILLET OF HALIBUT WITH GRAPES

4 lbs. halibut fillets
1 tsp. salt
1/2 tsp. pepper
3 tbsp. butter
1 cup canned seedless grapes, drained
Juice of 1 lemon

❖

Season halibut with salt and pepper. Cook in 2 tbsp. butter until tender. Saute grapes in remaining butter with lemon juice. Pour over halibut. Serves four.

HALIBUT FILLETS WITH GREEN GRAPES

2 lbs. halibut fillets
Salt and freshly ground pepper
Butter
1/2 lb. seedless green grapes
1/2 cup white wine
1 tsp. brandy
1/2 cup heavy cream

❖

Season fillets with salt and pepper. Place in buttered baking dish. Scatter grapes over halibut. Pour in white wine, brandy and heavy cream. Bake at 425° for 15 minutes or until halibut flakes. Baste frequently. Serves six.

BROILED HALIBUT WITH ANISE

2 lbs. halibut fillets
1/4 cup butter, melted
1/4 tsp. anise seed, crushed
1/2 cup dry white wine
1/8 tsp. salt
1 tbsp. parsley, chopped

❖

Saute anise seed in butter for one minute. Add wine and salt and simmer 5-10 minutes. Place fillets on oiled broiler pan and brush fillets with butter mixture. Broil 2 inches from heat about 6-10 minutes. Do not turn.

Place fillets on serving platter; pour remaining sauce over halibut. Garnish with parsley. Serves four.

HALIBUT
WITH ANISE SAUCE

2 lbs. cooked halibut, cut into bite-sized pieces
1/4 cup oil
3/4 cup minced scallions,
3 garlic cloves, minced
1/2 tsp. ground chili peppers
2 tsp. sugar
1 tsp. ground anise seed
2 tbsp. vinegar
1-1/2 cups water
2 tsp. anchovy paste

❖

Saute scallions in oil for five minutes. Stir in all but halibut and anchovy paste. Add halibut pieces and anchovy paste and cook 5 minutes. Serves eight.

BAKED HALIBUT
WITH MUSHROOMS

2 lbs. halibut steaks
Salt and pepper
3 tbsp. lemon juice
3 cups fine cracker crumbs
3/4 cup mayonnaise
1/2 lb. fresh mushrooms, sliced
1/2 cup green onions, sliced
3 tbsp. butter
2 tbsp. parsley, chopped
1/4 tsp. thyme leaves
Lemon wedges if desired

Season halibut with salt and pepper. Drizzle with lemon juice. Mix crumbs with 3/4 cup mayonnaise. Pat crumb mixture on both sides of steaks and place in a single layer in a buttered shallow baking dish. Bake, uncovered, in a 425° oven 10 to 15 minutes.

Saute butter, mushrooms and green onions until limp. Stir in parsley, thyme and salt and pepper to taste. Spoon mixture over fish; garnish with lemon wedges. Serves six.

HALIBUT
WITH SPICY TOMATO SAUCE

1-1/2 lb. halibut steaks
Salt and pepper
1/8 tsp. dried thyme
1 clove garlic, mashed
1 onion, chopped
2 tbsp. parsley, chopped
2 large tomatoes, sliced
1 cup white wine
1/2 tbsp. butter
1/2 tbsp. flour

❖

Season halibut with salt and pepper. Place steaks side by side in a casserole. Sprinkle with thyme, garlic, onion and parsley. Cover with tomato slices. Add wine to baking dish. Cover and bake at 350° for 25 to 30 minutes, or until halibut flakes. Remove halibut and keep warm. Reduce pan juices by half. Stir butter and flour into pan juices. Cook over low heat, stirring constantly, until sauce is thickened. Pour over fish. Serves four.

BROILED HALIBUT
WITH JULIENNED VEGETABLES

2 lbs. halibut fillets
1/4 seedless cucumber, peeled and sliced
 into 1/4 inch matchsticks
1 leek, trimmed of its roots and tough green
 leaves, halved lengthwise and rinsed
Dry white wine
3 tbsp. butter, melted
2 tbsp. bread crumbs
Salt to taste
Freshly ground white pepper
4 large leaves green-leaf or other lettuce,
 rinsed and dried
4 tbsp. fresh lemon juice

❖

Place cucumber and leek in a bowl of cold water. Preheat broiler. Pour 1/8 inch of wine into broiler pan and lay halibut in the wine. Spoon butter onto fish and sprinkile with salt and pepper. Broil fish for 4 minutes. sprinkle with bread crumbs and broil until the halibut is golden brown.

Blanch the vegetables in lightly salted water for 3 minutes. Blanch the lettuce leaves in the boiling water for 2 seconds. Lift them out and shake off water. Spread leaves on warmed serving platter and place the fish on top. Mix lemon juice with liquid in the broiler pan. Place little bunches of vegetables on top of the fish and pour the liquid from the broiler pan over all. Serves four.

BAKED HALIBUT
WITH ARTICHOKES

6 halibut steaks
2 shallots, peeled, seeded and chopped
1 jar (8 oz.) marinated artichoke hearts,
    drained and chopped
1/4 cup green onions, chopped
2 tbsp. parsley, chopped
2 tbsp. lemon juice

❖

Put halibut in baking dish. Stir together remaining
ingredients then pour over fish. Bake at 350° for 25
minutes, or until halibut flakes. Serves six.

BAKED HALIBUT
IN RAISIN AND NUT SAUCE

3 lbs. halibut fillets
1/2 cup olive or vegetable oil, plus oil for
    rubbing fish and preparing baking dish
5 carrots, sliced
1/2 cup celery, chopped
A few chopped celery leaves
1/4 cup currants or golden raisins
1/4 cup pignolia nuts
1 (8 ozs.) can tomato sauce
1 cup parsley, chopped
1 cup warm water
1/4 cup white wine
1 lemon, sliced
Salt and pepper to taste

❖

Rub halibut with oil and place in oiled baking dish. Combine remaining ingredients except sliced lemon and wine. Simmer 15 minutes and remove from heat. Add wine. Pour over fillets. Place slices of lemon on halibut. Salt and pepper to taste. Bake in 375° oven for about 1-1/2 hours or until halibut flakes. Baste as needed. Serves six.

HALIBUT WITH CIDER

1-1/2 to 2 lbs. halibut fillets
1 cup cider
1/2 cup water
2 tbsp. butter
1-1/2 tsp. flour
Squeeze of lemon juice
1 tbsp. parsley, chopped
2 tbsp. light cream
Salt and pepper

❖

Put halibut in a buttered baking dish. Pour cider and water over fish. Cover with buttered foil. and poach at 350° for 10-12 minutes. Remove fillets and keep warm. Strain the cooking liquid and reserve.

Melt butter in a saucepan. Stir in flour. Add reserved liquid. Bring to a boil and simmer 3-4 minutes. Add lemon juice, parsley, cream, and salt and pepper to taste. Spoon over fish. Serves four.

HALIBUT
WITH SNOW PEAS

2 lb. halibut fillets
1/2 cup water
5 tbsp. soy sauce
2 tbsp. sherry
3/4 cup snow peas

❖

Boil water, soy sauce and sherry. Add fish. Simmer until fillets flake. Remove fillets and keep warm. Boil snow peas in fish water until tender. Serve snow peas and halibut together. Serves four.

HALIBUT
A L'ORANGE

2 lbs. halibut fillets
1/2 cup concentrated orange juice (frozen)
2 tbsp. butter
1/2 tsp. salt
Dash of nutmeg

❖

Arrange halibut in single layer in buttered pan. Thaw orange juice and combine with butter and seasonings. Pour sauce over fish. Bake at 350° until halibut flakes easily. Serves four.

BAKED HALIBUT
WITH CHEESE SAUCE

2 lbs. halibut steaks
2 tbsp. lemon juice
4 tbsp. butter
4 tbsp. flour
2 cups hot milk
Salt and pepper
3/4 cup Cheddar cheese, grated
3 tbsp. Parmesan cheese, grated
2 hard cooked eggs, diced

❖

Broil halibut steaks about 15 minutes. Place in a buttered baking dish. Sprinkle with lemon juice.

Melt butter in saucepan over low heat. Stir in flour. Gradually add milk and cook, stirring constantly, until thickened. Season with salt and pepper. Pour sauce over fish, cover with grated cheeses, and bake uncovered at 350° for 20 minutes. Sprinkle with eggs before serving. Serves four.

HALIBUT FILLETS
IN TOMATOES AND PARSLEY

2 lbs. halibut fillets
1 large onion, finely chopped
1 large bunch parsley, chopped (discard stems)
1/4 cup olive oil
1 tsp. garlic, very finely chopped
4 medium tomatoes, peeled and cut in wedges
Juice of lemon
1/2 cup water
Salt and pepper

❖

Saute onions and parsley in olive oil until onions are tender. Stir in garlic and tomatoes and cook a few minutes. Add lemon juice, water, salt, and pepper and stir well. Add halibut and simmer for 10 to 15 minutes until it flakes. Serves four.

BAKED HALIBUT WITH CUCUMBER SAUCE

2 lbs. halibut steaks
1/2 cup celery, thinly sliced
1/2 cup onion, chopped
1/4 cup fresh parsley, chopped
1 tsp. salt
1/2 tsp. thyme
1/8 tsp. fresh-ground pepper
1 cup dry vermouth
3 egg yolks
2 tbsp. lemon juice
1/4 tsp. salt
1/8 tsp. dry mustard
1/2 cup margarine
1/2 cup cucumber, peeled and diced
1/2 cup heavy cream, whipped

❖

Place halibut in large shallow baking dish. Top with celery, onion, parsley, salt, thyme, pepper and vermouth. Bake uncovered in 350° oven until halibut flakes.

Mix in blender yolks, lemon juice, salt and mustard. In a small saucepan heat margarine until it foams. With blender on, add margarine to egg mixture in a slow, steady stream. Continue blending about 30 seconds or until thickened. Transfer sauce to top of double boiler over simmering water. Add cucumbers; stir gently until warmed through. Remove fish and vegetables to a warm serving dish. Fold whipped cream into sauce. Spoon over fish; serve immediately. Serves six.

BROILED HALIBUT
IN MAYONNAISE SAUCE

3-1/2 lbs. halibut fillets
1/2 cup mayonnaise
1 tbsp. Worcestershire sauce
2 tsp. lemon juice
1 tbsp. seafood seasoning
Salt and pepper to taste

❖

Salt and pepper fillets to taste. Place in a greased broiling pan. Combine mayonnaise, Worcestershire sauce, and lemon juice, and spread over the fish fillets. Sprinkle seasoning on top. Broil for 20 minutes, or until halibut flakes. Serves six.

CHEESE-TOPPED
HALIBUT

2 lbs. halibut fillets, in six pieces
2 tablespoons onion, grated
1-1/2 tsp. salt
1/8 tsp. pepper
2 large tomatoes, thinly sliced
1/4 cup melted butter
1 cup (4 ozs.) shredded Swiss cheese

Place fillets in greased baking dish. Sprinkle fish with onion and seasonings. Arrange tomato slices over halibut. Pour butter over tomatoes. Broil about 4 inches from heat for 10 minutes, or until halibut flakes. Remove from heat. Sprinkle with cheese. Broil 2 to 3 minutes longer or until cheese is melted. Serves six.

HALIBUT PROVENCALE WITH TOMATOES AND CHEESE

2 lbs. halibut fillets
Garlic powder
Paprika
1 can (1 lb.) stewed tomatoes,
  drained and chopped
1/2 cup green onions, chopped
4 tbsp. parsley, chopped
4 tbsp. grated Parmesan cheese
8 thin lemon slices
Salt and pepper to taste

❖

Arrange fillets in large baking dish. Sprinkle with spices. Layer tomatoes, green onion, parsley and cheese evenly over fish. Lay lemon slices on top. Bake at 350° until halibut flakes. Serves six.

HALIBUT
IN WINE SAUCE

1-1/2 lbs. halibut fillets
1/4 cup onion, chopped
1 clove garlic, minced
2 tbsp. butter or margarine
1 small tomato, chopped (1/2 cup)
1/3 cup dry white wine
1 tbsp. parsley, snipped
1/2 tsp. salt
Dash pepper
1/3 cup milk
2 tsp. cornstarch

❖

Saute onion and garlic in butter until tender. Add fish, tomato, wine, parsley, salt and pepper. Cover; cook over low heat 10-12 minutes or until halibut flakes. Remove fillets; keep warm.

Blend milk and cornstarch; add to skillet. Cook and stir till thickened and bubbly. Cook 1-2 minutes more. Pour over halibut. Serves four.

ORANGE-GLAZED HALIBUT

1-1/2 lbs. halibut steaks
2 tbsp. green onion, chopped
1 tbsp. butter or margarine
4 tsp. cornstarch
1 cup orange juice
1 tsp. instant chicken bouillon granules
1/2 tsp. salt
1 orange, peeled, sectioned, and diced

❖

Place halibut in greased baking dish. Saute onion in butter till tender. Blend in cornstarch. Add orange juice, bouillon and salt. Cook and stir till thickened and bubbly. Stir in diced orange; pour over fish. Bake in 350° oven for 20 minutes or until halibut flakes. Spoon sauce over fish. Serves four.

HALIBUT
WITH TOMATO TOPPING

3 small halibut steaks
1 tbsp. lemon juice
Salt and pepper
1 medium onion, finely chopped
1 large tomato, peeled with seeds removed
2 tbsp. oil
2 tbsp. green pepper, chopped

❖

Mix lemon juice with sufficient water to make a poaching stock for halibut steaks. Season steaks with salt and pepper. Place in a shallow baking dish. Pour the stock round and cover with foil. Place in a 350° oven for 15 minutes.

Saute onion and green pepper in oil until limp. Add chopped tomato. Cook, stirring gently, until heated through. Drain off stock from fish if necessary using paper towels. Spoon the topping over fish and serve hot. Serves three.

HALIBUT
WITH MUSTARD SAUCE

8 small halibut fillets
2 tbsp. mild mustard
Salt and pepper
1/2 cup water
1/2 cup dry white wine
1 tbsp. parsley, chopped
1 tbsp. butter
1/2 cup whipping cream

❖

Spread mustard on one side of fillets. Season with salt and pepper. Roll up each fillet with the mustard on the inside. Stand the halibut rolls upright in a buttered baking dish. Pour water and wine around the fillets. Sprinkle with parsley and dot with butter. Bake in a 350° oven for 20 minutes.

Arrange fillets on a warm serving platter. Reduce the cooking liquid to half its volume by fast boiling, then stir in the remaining cream. Season with salt and pepper. Serves eight.

HALIBUT STEAKS
WITH MACADAMIA SAUCE

12 oz. halibut steaks cut 1/2 inch thick
1-1/2 tbsp. fresh lime juice
1 tbsp. flour
1/2 tsp. salt
1/8 tsp. ground black pepper
1 tbsp. butter
1 cup heavy cream or half and half
3 tbsp. water
1/4 cup chopped macadamia nuts
Lime slices and parsley

❖

Sprinkle both sides of fish with lime juice and let stand for 10 minutes. Combine flour, 1/4 tsp. salt and black pepper. Dip halibut in flour mixture; shake off excess. Melt butter and add fish. Cook until fish flakes easily, turning once. Remove to a warm serving platter and set aside.

Add cream, water, macadamia nuts and remaining 1/4 tsp. salt to pan. Cook and stir over low heat, scraping bottom of pan, until sauce is lightly browned and thickened. Spoon over fish. Garnish with lime and parsley. Serves two.

WINE-POACHED HALIBUT

1-1/2 lb. halibut steaks
3/4 cup dry white wine or water
1/2 cup water
1/2 cup fresh mushrooms, sliced
1/4 cup celery, thinly sliced
1 clove garlic, minced
1/2 tsp. dried mint, crushed
1/4 tsp. salt
1/8 tsp. pepper
Chopped pimiento
Lemon wedges

❖

   Combine wine, water, mushrooms, celery, garlic, mint, salt, and pepper. Bring to boil; reduce heat. Simmer, covered, for 5 minutes. Add halibut and simmer, covered, till fish flakes. Remove the fish and keep it warm.

   Boil vegetable mixture gently, uncovered, for 3 to 6 minutes or till reduced to 1/4 to 2/3 cup. Spoon atop steaks. Sprinkle with chopped pimiento. Garnish with lemon wedges. Serves four.

STEAMED
HALIBUT FILLETS

1-1/2 pounds halibut fillet
1/2 tsp. salt
1/8 tsp. white pepper
1/2 tsp. sugar
1 tbsp. white wine
1/2 tbsp. soy sauce
1 tbsp. vegetable oil
1 tbsp. grated gingerroot,
1 scallion, cut on the diagonal into 1-inch pieces

❖

Dry fillets with paper towels. Arrange fillets on a plate and season with salt and pepper. Mix sugar, white wine, soy sauce, oil, ginger and scallions. Pour mixture over halibut. Place fish in a steamer. Cover and steam until the fish flakes easily, about 7-10 minutes. Serves four.

PARMESAN
HALIBUT

2 lbs. halibut fillets
Salt and pepper
Butter
4 thin slices of Parmesan cheese
1/4 cup fish stock or chicken broth

Place fillets in a buttered skillet. Season with salt and pepper and dot with butter. Brown gently on both sides. Top each fillet with slice of cheese and sprinkle on the stock. Cover and simmer slowly for about 5 minutes until the cheese melts. Serves four.

SPICY HALIBUT FILLETS

3 lbs. halibut fillets
2 garlic cloves, minced
1/2 tsp. ground chili pepper
1/8 tsp. ground cuminseed
3/4 tsp. salt
1/4 tsp. pepper
4 tbsp. butter
1/2 cup buttermilk
2 tsp. lemon juice

❖

Mix garlic, chile, cuminseed, salt and pepper. Rub into fillets. Melt butter and brown fillets well on both sides. Add milk and lemon juice. Cook over low heat until liquid is absorbed. Serves six.

CORN BREAD
HALIBUT BAKE

1 lb. halibut fillets
1-1/2 cups cornmeal
3/4 tsp. baking soda
1/4 cup onion, finely chopped
2 tbsp. green chili peppers, chopped
1 cup buttermilk
2 eggs
1/4 cup shortening, melted
1/4 cup butter, melted
2 tbsp. prepared mustard
Paprika

❖

Cut fillets into 1x4-inch strips. Set aside. In a large mixing bowl stir together cornmeal and soda. Add onion and chili peppers. Beat together buttermilk and eggs. Stir into cornmeal mixture along with shortening. Spread batter in greased 7-1/2 x 12 x 2-inch baking dish. Place halibut in rows atop batter; press into batter. Stir together butter and mustard. Spread over fish. Sprinkle with paprika. Bake in 450° oven 20 minutes. Serves four.

HALIBUT-POTATO BAKE

1 lb. halibut steaks
Salt and pepper to taste
1 lb. small new potatoes, cooked
1 tbsp. butter
2 tbsp. dry white wine
1/3 cup sour cream
1 tsp. lemon juice
1/2 tsp. paprika

❖

Season halibut with salt and pepper and place with potatoes in greased baking dish. Dot with butter; sprinkle with wine. Bake at 425° until fish flakes easily. Remove fish and potatoes and keep warm.

Drain juices from pan into saucepan. Combine with sour cream, lemon juice, paprika, and 1/8 tsp. pepper. Cook and stir until hot; do not boil. Pour over halibut and potatoes. Serves two.

TASTY HALIBUT FILLETS

2 lbs. halibut fillets
1/2 tsp. garlic salt
1/2 cup plus 2 tsp. instant mashed potato flakes
1 cup chicken broth
1 tbsp. green onion, chopped
2 teaspoons parsley, chopped
3 tbsp. butter

✜

Fry fillets in butter until browned. Drain on absorbent paper and keep warm. Add garlic salt, potato flakes and broth to pan and simmer for 1 or 2 minutes or until thick. Stir constantly. Pour sauce over halibut. Garnish with parsley and green onion. Serves six.

STUFFED HALIBUT FILLETS

1-1/2 lbs. halibut fillet
5 slices bacon, cut in half
1/4 cup almonds, slivered
3 green onions split lengthwise and in 2: lengths
3 tbsp. vegetable oil
1/4 cup water
1 tbsp. cornstarch
1 tbsp. soy sauce
1/2 tbsp. brandy
Salt and pepper to taste
1 tbsp. bottled oyster sauce

Fry half-slices of bacon. Remove from pan and drain on paper toweling. Fry almonds in bacon fat, stirring them as they cook, until they turn golden brown. Drain. Discard bacon fat and wipe pan. Heat oil in skillet and add onions. When they become limp, remove them from pan. Combine water, 1 tbsp. cornstarch, soy sauce, and brandy in a bowl and set aside.

Cut fillet into 3 x 2 x 1/2" strips. Flatten them out on waxed paper covered with cornstarch. Sprinkle with salt and pepper. Place nuts, bacon, and green onion on each piece of fish, then roll and fasten with wooden cocktail picks. Saute halibut rolls gently for about 3 minutes, turning them carefully. Add oyster sauce and continue cooking for 2 minutes more. Pour in soy mixture and cook, turning and moving fish around in the pan until sauce thickens and the rolls are coated with sauce. Transfer halibut rolls to a warm platter. Serves four.

LEMON
BROILED HALIBUT

2 lbs. halibut steaks
1 tbsp. onion, grated
2 tbsp. lemon juice
4 tbsp. butter, melted
1 tsp. salt
Dash of pepper
1/4 tsp. thyme
Paprika and parsley
Lemon wedges from 1 lemon

❖

Place steaks on greased broiler pan. Combine onion, lemon juice, salt, pepper and thyme with butter. Baste steaks with half of the butter mixture. Place halibut 2 to 4 inches from broiler unit and broil for 5 minutes. Turn, baste with remaining sauce and continue broiling until cooked. Garnish with paprika and parsley, and lemon wedges. Serves four.

ELEGANT
HALIBUT

1 lb. halibut steaks
Salt
1 tbsp. butter or margarine
1 can (2-1/2 oz.) mushrooms, drained or 1 cup
    fresh mushrooms
1/2 cup sour cream
1 tbsp. dry sherry
Paprika

Sprinkle halibut with salt. Place in greased baking disk. Bake at 425° for 5 minutes. Saute mushrooms in butter until tender. Remove from heat; add sour cream and sherry. Spoon sauce over halibut. Sprinkle with paprika. Return to oven and bake at 375° for 20 minutes or until halibut flakes. Serves four.

BAKED HALIBUT AND DRESSING

2 lbs. halibut fillets
3 tbsp. butter
1/2 cup onion, chopped
1/2 cup mushrooms, chopped
1/4 cup celery, chopped
2 cups soft bread crumbs
Salt, pepper and tarragon to taste
Lemon juice
4 tomatoes, peeled and sliced

✜

Saute in butter the onions, mushrooms and celery until tender. Remove from heat and stir in bread crumbs and seasonings. In a greased baking dish layer fillets. Season fillets with lemon juice and cover with dressing. Top with tomato slices. Bake uncovered at 375° for 35-40 minutes. Garnish with lemon slices and tarragon sprigs. Serves four.

HALIBUT PARMESAN

2-1/2 lbs. halibut fillets
3 tbsp. each flour and yellow cornmeal
1/2 tsp. each garlic salt and dry mustard
1/4 tsp. each dry rosemary leaves and pepper
3 tbsp. butter, melted
3 tbsp. milk
Paprika
1/4 to 1/3 cup grated Parmesan cheese
Lemon wedges

❖

Mix flour, cornmeal, garlic salt, mustard, rosemary and pepper.

Dip fish in milk, drain briefly, then roll in coating mixture to cover evenly. Arrange fish in baking dish and cover with melted butter. Sprinkle fish lightly with paprika and half of the grated Parmesan cheese. Bake at 350° until fish flakes easily.

Halfway through baking time, turn fish over;sprinkle lightly with paprika and the remaining Parmesan cheese. Garnish with a lemon wedge. Serves four.

HALIBUT
AND PINEAPPLE

2 lbs. halibut fillets
2 tsp. salt
1/4 tsp. pepper
1/4 tsp. ground ginger
1 can (20 oz.) pineapple chunks, drained
1 green pepper, cut in strips
6 tomato slices

❖

Season fillets with salt, pepper and ginger. Cut six 12-inch squares of aluminum foil and grease them. On each square place a portion of halibut, 6 pineapple chunks, 4 strips of green pepper and 1 slice of tomato. Seal foil. Place packages on a baking pan. Bake at 450° for 20 to 25 minutes. Serves six.

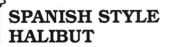

SPANISH STYLE HALIBUT

4 small halibut fillets
1 medium onion, chopped
1 clove garlic, crushed
4 tomatoes, peeled, seeded and chopped
1 tbsp. olive oil
1/4 cup walnuts, chopped
2 tsp. orange rind, grated
2 tbsp. orange juice
1/2 cup dry white wine
Salt and pepper
Orange slices to garnish

❖

Saute onion and garlic in olive oil until tender. Stir in chopped tomato, walnuts, orange rind, juice, and white wine. Bring to simmering point, then add fillets. Simmer gently until tender. Arrange halibut on a warm platter. Season sauce with salt and pepper and pour over fish. Garnish with orange slices. Serves four.

EASY HALIBUT STEAKS MEUNIERE

1-1/2 lbs. halibut steaks
1 envelope (about 1 oz.) white-sauce mix
4 tbsp. butter
1/4 cup lemon juice
2 tbsp. almonds, sliced

Sprinkle halibut steaks with white-sauce mix. Melt 2 tbsp. butter in large skillet. Saute halibut steaks 3 minutes on each side. Add remaining butter to skillet. Stir in lemon juice. Heat a few minutes. Sprinkle with almonds. Serves four.

BROILED HALIBUT STEAKS WITH ROSEMARY

2 medium halibut steaks
1/4 cup olive oil
Freshly ground pepper to taste
2 tsp. fresh rosemary (or 1 tsp. dried)

✤

Brush steaks with olive oil and pepper. Press rosemary into halibut on both sides. Broil steaks 6 to 7 minutes on each side, turning once. These steaks may also be baked in a preheated oven at 400° for 15 to 20 minutes without being turned. Serves two.

BAKED
FILLET OF HALIBUT

2 lbs. halibut fillets
1/2 cup milk
1 tsp. salt
1/4 tsp. pepper
1 cup fine sourdough French bread crumbs
2 cans condensed cream of mushroom soup,
   undiluted
3/4 cup dry sherry
3/4 cup Chablis
1 tsp. soy sauce
1 tsp. teriyaki sauce
1 tsp. white vinegar
3 tbsp. lemon juice

❖

Combine milk with salt and pepper and stir until salt is dissolved. Dip halibut in milk, then gently press each fillet in crumbs, coating both sides well. Dry them on waxed paper while making sauce.

Heat mushroom soup in a saucepan until it boils. Combine sherry, Chablis, soy and teriyaki sauces, vinegar, and lemon juice and stir into mushroom soup. Heat, stirring, to a boil, then pour half of the sauce into a large shallow baking dish. Arrange fillets on top. Bake at 350° for 7-10 minutes, or until coating turns brown.

Remove from oven and pour over remaining sauce, then return dish to oven to bake for another 10 minutes. Serves four.

BARBECUED HALIBUT STEAKS

4 halibut steaks
1 small onion, minced
1/2 green pepper, chopped
3 tbsp. butter
1/2 cup chili sauce
1/2 cup catsup
Juice of 2 lemons
2 tbsp. brown sugar
1/2 cup water
1 tsp. dry mustard
1 tbsp. Worcestershire sauce
1/2 tsp. each salt and pepper

❖

Saute onion and green pepper in butter. Add remaining ingredients except halibut and simmer for 10 minutes. Broil halibut in preheated broiler until done, brushing from time to time with sauce. Serves four.

SESAME
HALIBUT BAKE

6 halibut steaks
1 cup sesame-seed paste (tahini paste)
4 garlic cloves, minced
Juice of 2 lemons
Salt to taste
1/2 cup water
1/2 cup toasted pine nuts
1/4 cup olive oil
1/4 cup lemon juice
Salt and freshly ground pepper to taste
1/4 cup vegetable oil
2 large onions, sliced, separated in rings

❖

Combine sesame-seed paste, garlic, lemon juice and salt in blender. Process until smooth. Gradually blend in water. Set aside.

Rinse fish and pat dry. Place in a baking dish. Sprinkle fish with olive oil, lemon juice, salt and pepper. Turn fish to coat well. Cover and marinate 2 hours or longer in refrigerator.

Bake at 350° uncovered, basting as necessary until halibut flakes. Saute onions in oil until onions are golden brown. Pour sesame-seed sauce over fish. Top with browned onion rings. Sprinkle with toasted pine nuts. Serves six.

HALIBUT
PEASANT STYLE

2 lbs. halibut fillets
1/4 tsp. paprika
2 tbsp. melted butter
1 tsp. fennel seed, crushed
1 tsp. parsley flakes
1/4 tsp. dried thyme
1 tbsp. lemon juice
1/2 cup dry white wine

❖

Arrange fillets in baking pan and sprinkle with paprika. Combine remaining ingredients. Pour over halibut. Bake in a 375° oven 20 minutes or until fish flakes. Baste frequently. Serves six.

BAKED HALIBUT FILLETS

2 lbs. halibut fillets, in six pieces
1/2 lb. butter
2 onions, chopped
3 cups bread crumbs
4 egg yolks, beaten
2 tbsp. heavy cream
1/2 tsp. grated nutmeg
1/2 cup sherry
1 tsp. salt
1 tsp. pepper

✤

Saute onions in half of the butter until tender. Add bread crumbs and cook over low heat, stirring for 2 minutes. Remove from heat and stir in the yolks. Add cream, nutmeg, and half the sherry, salt and pepper. Divide into 6 parts. Roll a fillet around each part and fasten with food picks or poultry pins. Melt remaining butter, add fillets, and sprinkle with rest of sherry and salt and pepper. Bake at 400° for 30 minutes, basting frequently Serves six.

EXQUISITE HALIBUT STEAKS

2 lbs. halibut steaks
Juice of 1 lemon
1/2 tsp. salt
1/8 tsp. pepper
1/2 tsp. dried marjoram
1/2 cup green onions, thinly sliced
1/2 cup celery, chopped
2 tbsp. butter
1/2 tbsp. caraway seeds
1/2 cup white wine

❖

Put halibut steaks in shallow baking dish. Squeeze on lemon juice. Season with salt, pepper and marjoram. Let marinate for one hour, turning once. Saute onions and celery in butter until tender. Spread over fish steaks. Sprinkle on caraway seeds. Bake at 400° for 10 minutes.

Add wine and bake for 10 minutes more. Serves six.

GREAT HALIBUT BAKED IN FOIL

2 pounds halibut fillets
1 tsp. green onion, chopped
1-1/2 cups soft bread crumbs
1 egg, well beaten
2 tbsp. butter
1/2 cup condensed asparagus soup
8 large mushroom caps, fresh or canned

❖

Mix together onion and crumbs. Add egg and 1 tbsp. melted butter. Spread on fillets, then roll them up and fasten with a toothpick. Place each fillet on a greased square of aluminum foil large enough to wrap completely. Spoon asparagus soup over each fillet. Top with a mushroom cap and a dot of butter. Fold foil around each fillet. Bake at 400° for 25-30 minutes. Serves four.

HERB-BAKED HALIBUT

2 lb. halibut fillets
1 tbsp. butter
1 cup milk
2 tbsp. flour
1/4 tsp. salt
1/4 tsp. garlic salt
1/8 tsp. pepper
1/8 tsp. dried thyme, crushed
1/4 cup green onion, chopped
Dash dried oregano, crushed
Paprika

❖

   Place halibut in baking dish and dot with butter. Blend milk and flour. Cook over medium heat, stirring constantly, till sauce thickens and bubbles. Cook and stir one minute longer. Stir in salt, garlic salt, pepper, thyme, oregano, and chopped green onion. Pour sauce over halibut. Sprinkle lightly with paprika. Bake, uncovered, at 350° for 20 to 25 minutes. Serves four.

BAKED
HALIBUT FILLETS

2 pounds halibut fillets
2 tbsp. butter
1/2 tsp. salt
1/8 tsp. pepper
4 green onions, thinly sliced
4 tsp. minced herbs, parsley, tarragon, chervil
1 cup fresh bread crumbs
1/3 cup dry vermouth
3 tbsp. butter for topping

❖

Melt butter in bottom of baking pan. Season fillets with salt and pepper and dip them in butter. Spread herbs and onions in bottom of baking pan and place fish on top of them in a single layer. Cover with bread crumbs. Sprinkle vermouth over all and dot with 3 tablespoons butter. Bake uncovered at 375° until crumbs are browned and fish flakes. Serves six.

HALIBUT
ROYALE

6 halibut steaks
3 tbsp. lemon juice
1 tsp. salt
1/2 tsp. paprika
1/2 cup onion, chopped
2 tbsp. butter
1 green pepper, cut into strips

Combine lemon juice, salt and paprika. Add halibut steaks and marinate for one hour, turning steaks after 30 minutes. Saute onions in butter till tender. Place steaks in greased baking dish. Top with green pepper strips and sprinkle with onion. Bake at 450° for 10 minutes. Serves six.

BAKED
FILLETS OF HALIBUT

4 halibut fillets
1 large can chopped mushrooms
4 cups potatoes, diced
2 tbsp. butter
1 tsp. salt
1/2 tsp. pepper
Dash of paprika
2/3 cup white wine
1 cup sour cream
Lemon slices
Parsley sprigs

❖

Place potatoes and mushrooms in a baking dish. Dot with half of the butter, salt, pepper, and paprika. Pour wine and half of the sour cream in dish and season with remaining salt, pepper, paprika, and the rest of the sour cream. Bake at 375° for 45 minutes or until halibut flakes. Garnish with lemon and parsley. Serves four.

HALIBUT AND LAMB CASSEROLE

4 halibut fillets
4 tbsp. olive oil
2 cloves garlic, pressed
2 medium onions, sliced
1 lb. lamb, ground
1 lb. tomatoes, peeled and quartered
1/2 tsp. ground cumin
1 tsp. paprika
Salt and pepper
Juice of 2 lemons
Lemon wedges

❖

Heat oil in a heavy frying pan and brown fillets on both sides. Lift fish fillets out and place them in a baking dish.

In the same frying pan, saute garlic and onion until tender. Stir in lamb, tomatoes, spices, and seasoning to taste. Gently fry until meat is browned. Pour contents of pan over fillets and squeeze the lemon juice over them. Cover baking dish and bake at 325° for 1-1/2 hours. Garnish with lemon wedges. Serves four.

BAKED HALIBUT FILLETS

2 lbs. halibut fillets
1 onion, chopped
Salt
1 tsp. prepared mustard
Dash of Tabasco
1 tsp. Worcestershire sauce
2 tsp. lemon juice
Few drops of white vinegar
1 tomato, diced
3 parsley sprigs, minced
Pinch of curry powder
Pinch of paprika

❖

Arrange onion on bottom of baking dish. Season fillets with salt and place on onions. Mix mustard, Tabasco, 1/2 tsp. Worcestershire, lemon juice and vinegar and spread on fillets. Cover fillets just to the top with hot water. Bake at 350° for 15 minutes or until halibut flakes.

Melt butter. Add tomato, parsley, curry powder, paprika and remaining Worcestershire. Stir and pour over halibut. Serves four.

BASIC
HALIBUT ROAST

2-1/2 lb. halibut roast
1/4 tsp. thyme, crushed
1/8 tsp. each crushed rosemary, salt and pepper
1 medium onion, thinly sliced
1 carrot, chopped
2 tbsp. lemon juice
2 tbsp. butter, melted

❖

Combine thyme, rosemary, salt and pepper. Season halibut with mixture. Place half of vegetables in baking dish; place roast on vegetables. Top halibut with remaining vegetables. Drizzle with lemon juice and butter. Bake at 450° until halibut flakes easily. Serves six.

HALIBUT FILLETS
AU GRATIN

1 lb. halibut fillets
2 tbsp. fine cracker crumbs
1 cup canned tomatoes with liquid
2 tbsp. onion, chopped
1/4 tsp. salt
Freshly ground pepper
1 tbsp. butter
1/4 cup Cheddar cheese, shredded

Sprinkle lightly greased baking dish with crumbs. Arrange halibut on dish. Combine tomatoes onion, salt and pepper and pour over fillets. Dot with butter. Bake at 375° for 20 minutes. Sprinkle with cheese and return to oven until cheese melts. Serves four.

HALIBUT ORANGE FILLETS

3 lbs. halibut fillets
4 tbsp. butter
1 tbsp. minced onion
2/3 cup orange juice
1/3 cup dry white wine
1 tsp. grated orange rind
Segments of 2 large oranges, peeled
Milk
Flour
Salt and white pepper

❖

Dip fillets into milk, then dust with flour. Saute in 3 tbsp. butter until well browned on both sides and halibut flakes easily. Season with salt and pepper and keep warm. Cook minced onion in butter remaining in pan until tender.

Stir in orange juice, wine and grated rind. Season with salt and pepper and simmer for 5 minutes. Strain sauce into another pan and blend in remaining 1 tbsp. butter. Add orange segments and heat through. Arrange segments around fillets and pour sauce over. Serves six.

FOIL-BAKED HALIBUT

2 lbs. halibut fillets
1 medium onion, sliced
3 tbsp. mayonnaise
Juice of one lime
2 tbsp. butter
Dash of Worcestershire sauce
Dash of soy sauce

❖

Arrange halibut on foil and top with onion. Mix remaining ingredients. Pour sauce over fillets and dot with butter. Seal the foil and bake on coals (or in 350° oven) for 20 to 25 minutes. Serves four.

TOMIE'S GOLDEN HALIBUT

1-1/2 lbs. halibut fillets
Seasoned bread crumbs
1/2 cup mayonnaise
I-1/2 tsp. lemon juice
1/2 cup low fat yogurt
I egg white, beatened stiff
1/4 cup green onion, chopped
1/4 cup almonds, sliced
dash paprika

Dip fillets in crumbs and place in a greased baking dish. Combine in a bowl mayonnaise and lemon juice; add yogurt and blend well. Fold in egg whites. Sprinkle fillets with onions and spoon mayonnaise mixture on top of the fillets. Sprinkle with almonds and paprika. Bake in a preheated 400° oven for 20 minutes or until halibut flakes. Serves four.

SOUR CREAM HALIBUT

2 lbs. halibut fillets
1 cup sour cream
2 tbsp. butter
2 tbsp. water
1 tbsp. parsley, minced
Salt and pepper

✛

Placed fillets in greased dish. Barely cover bottom with water. Season with salt and pepper and bake at 400° for 15 to 20 minutes. Baste 2 or 3 times.

Scald cream in a double boiler with butter and water. Add parsley and pour over fish. Return to oven for 5 minutes. Sprinkle with paprika. Serves four.

CONNIE'S
BAKED HALIBUT

4 halibut steaks
1 onion, sliced
2 tbsp. butter
2 tsp. lemon juice
2/3 cup mayonnaise
1/3 cup sour cream
1 cup toasted bread crumbs
Salt and pepper

✣

Saute onions in butter until tender. Cover bottom of baking dish with onions and butter. Lay fish on top and cover with sour cream and mayonnaise mixture. Top with crumbs and bake at 375° for 20 minutes or until halibut flakes. Serves four.

HALIBUT
PROVENCALE

2 lbs. halibut fillets
1 tsp. salt
1/4 tsp. pepper
Juice of 1 lemon
1/4 cup flour
2 tbsp. olive oil
1 shallot, chopped
3 tbsp. butter
1 garlic clove, chopped fine
2 large tomatoes

Season halibut with salt and pepper; sprinkle with lemon juice. Dip in flour. Heat olive oil in skillet and cook fillets until both sides are brown. Remove and keep warm.

Cook shallot, butter, and garlic 2 minutes. Skin tomatoes, chop, drain off juice, and add pulp to garlic mixture. Stir and cook 5 minutes. Pour over halibut. Serves four.

GRILLED HALIBUT

1 lb. halibut fillets
2 tbsp. soy sauce
1 tsp. lemon juice
salt and pepper
1/2 cup sour cream
1/2 cup cornflakes, fine
2 tbsp. sesame seeds, toasted

❖

Brush halibut with a mixture of soy sauce, lemon juice, salt and pepper. Coat both sides of halibut with sour cream. Combine cornflakes and seasame seeds; roll fillets in the mixture. Place fillets in a wire basket and broil over medium coals for ten minutes; turn only once. Serves four.

FRIED
HALIBUT STEAKS

4 halibut steaks
2 tsp. lemon juice
1 egg beaten frothy
Flour
salt and pepper
4 tbsp. olive oil
2 garlic cloves

❖

Drip lemon juice over halibut and let stand ten minutes. Salt and pepper steaks and dip into beaten egg; then into flour. Heat oil with garlic and cook until garlic turns brown; remove garlic and cook steaks over medium high heat until brown on both sides about nine minutes. Serves four.

FRIED HALIBUT

1 lb. halibut fillet, two pieces
1 quart milk
1 tsp. salt
1/2 tsp. white pepper
1/4 cup flour
1/2 tsp. salt
1/4 tsp. pepper
1 cup oil
1/2 cup margarine
1 tbsp. chives, minced
1 lemon, halved
1/2 cup butter, melted
1 tsp. parsley, minced

❖

Soak halibut in milk, salt and white pepper for 24 hours. Drain and roll in flour mixed with salt and black pepper. Cook halibut in oil for 10 minutes until brown.

Pour oil from skillet; add margarine and chives and turn halibut. Drizzle lemon juice over fillets and simmer for 20 minutes. Remove fillets and place on platter. Add melted butter and parsley. Serves two.

VALDEZ HALIBUT

8 halibut steaks
1/8 tsp. cinnamon, ground
2 tbsp. chili powder
1/2 tsp. sugar
10 green olives, sliced
3 potatoes, boiled and diced
4 slices bread, sauteed and cut in strips
1/2 cup olive oil
1 tsp. onions, minced
1 garlic clove, minced
2 cups tomato sauce
2 peppercorns, ground
2 whole cloves

❖

Saute onions and garlic in half of the oil. Add tomato sauce and spices and cook for 30 minutes. Add sugar and olives. Sautee the steaks in the rest of the oil until halibut flakes. When the halibut is done, add to the sauce with the potatoes. Garnish with bread sticks. Serves eight.

SPICY
BAKED HALIBUT

2 lbs. halibut fillets
3 tbsp. butter
1 green pepper, chopped
3 tomatoes, fresh or canned, chopped
2 tsp. salt
1/4 tsp. oregano
1 clove garlic, minced
1/2 tsp. chili powder
2 tbsp. minced parsley
1/4 cup sliced green olives
1 tbsp. capers
1 cup port or other red wine

❖

Saute green pepper in butter until tender. Add remaining ingredients except wine to green pepper and cook 5 minutes.

Add wine and heat a minute longer. Pour sauce into shallow baking dish. Arrange halibut in dish, spooning some sauce over top. Bake at 350° until fish flakes. Serves six.

HALIBUT
POT ROAST

3 lbs. halibut roast
1 cup flour
1/2 cup oil
6 carrots
6 medium onions
2 cups celery, chopped
6 medium potatoes
2 cloves garlic, finely chopped
2 tsp. salt
1/2 tsp. pepper
2 cups water

❖

Roll halibut in flour and brown in oil on all sides in a large frying pan. Place vegetables around halibut and season with salt and pepper. Add water, cover and bake at 350° until halibut flakes.

Remove roast and vegetables to hot platter. Thicken liquid in pan and serve over halibut. Serves six.

BAKED
HALIBUT ROAST

4 lbs. halibut roast
1-1/2 tsp. salt
Dash of pepper
1/4 cup butter, melted
4 slices bacon

Season roast with salt and pepper and place in greased baking pan. Brush with melted butter and place bacon slices over top. Bake at 350° until fish flakes. Serves six.

SKILLET HALIBUT

1 lb. halibut fillets
1 onion, sliced
2 tbsp. butter
1/4 cup lemon juice
2 cups zucchini, sliced
1/2 cup swiss cheese, shredded
1/2 cup tomato, chopped
1/2 tsp. oreqano leaves
1 cup mushrooms, sliced

✤

Saute onion in butter until tender. Add fillets and other inqredients except cheese and tomatoes and simmer for ten minutes. Top with cheese and tomatoes and simmer for another 3 minutes until cheese melts. Servers four.

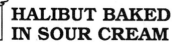

HALIBUT BAKED IN SOUR CREAM

2 lbs. halibut fillets, cut into 1-inch cubes
1/4 cup flour
2 tsp. salt
1/4 tsp. pepper
1 cup milk
2 cups coarse soft bread crumbs (4 slices)
1/4 cup butter
1 tsp. dillweed
1 carton (8 ozs.) sour cream
1 lemon, sliced
Parsley

❖

Coat halibut with mixture of flour, salt and pepper. Arrange in single layer in baking dish. Pour milk over and bake at 350° for 45 minutes.

Brown crumbs in butter in a medium-size skillet. Stir dill into sour cream. Remove fish from oven. Spoon the cream mixture over and top with toasted crumbs. Bake 10 minutes longer, or until the sour cream is set. Garnish with the lemon slices and parsley. Serves six.

CREAMED SMOKED HALIBUT

2 lbs. smoked halibut
6 tbsp. butter, melted
1-1/2 tsp. flour
1 tsp. dry mustard
1-1/2 cups milk
3/4 cup bread crumbs

❖

Steam smoked halibut over low heat for 15 minutes. Remove and cut into serving pieces. Place halibut in a greased baking dish. Melt butter and blend in flour and mustard. Slowly add milk and cook until thickened. Pour over halibut. Mix bread crumbs and remaining butter. Sprinkle on top of halibut and bake in a preheated 350° oven for 20 minutes. Serves six.

HALIBUT
RICE CASSEROLE

2 cups cooked halibut, flaked
2 cups cooked rice
1/2 cup onion, chopped
1/4 cup green pepper, diced
2 tbsp. butter
1 can (10 oz.) condensed tomato soup
1/2 cup milk
2 cups potato chips, coarsely crushed

❖

Add halibut to cooked rice. Saute onion and green pepper in butter until tender. Add to fish and rice and mix lightly. Blend soup with milk.

Place 1 cup of potato chips in bottom of a greased 2-quart casserole. Cover with alternate layers of fish and sauce. Top with rest of potato chips and bake at 350° for 25-30 minutes. Serves six.

SMOKED
HALIBUT CASSEROLE

1/2 lb. halibut fillets, cut into 1-inch pieces
1/2 lb. smoked halibut, cut into 1-inch pieces
1 tbsp. butter
1/2 tsp. salt
1/4 tsp. pepper
3 tbsp. fresh dill, chopped or 1 tsp. dried
3/4 cup light cream
4 tbsp. Swiss cheese, shredded
2 tbsp. bread crumbs

❖

Place a layer of halibut fillets in baking dish. Sprinkle with salt, pepper, and dill. Top with a layer of smoked fish. Repeat. Pour cream over the casserole. Sprinkle with cheese and bread crumbs. Bake 1/2 hour at 400° until the surface is crisp and brown. Serves four.

CURRIED
HALIBUT CASSEROLE

1-1/2 lbs. cooked halibut, flaked
1 package (8 oz.) cooked noodles
1-1/2 tsp. curry powder
2 tbsp. melted butter
1/2 cup milk
1 can (10 oz.) cream of mushroom soup
1 cup grated cheese

❖

Place cooked noodles in a greased casserole. Cover with flaked fish. Combine curry, butter, milk and soup. Add to casserole and sprinkle with cheese. Bake in a 350° oven for 30 minutes. Serves six.

HALIBUT
AND RED CABBAGE

3 lbs. halibut, cut into serving pieces
1 head of red cabbage, shredded
1 onion, minced
1 tbsp. butter
1/2 tbsp. flour
1 cup red wine
Salt and pepper
Juice of 1/2 lemon
1 tsp. sugar

Blanch halibut in boiling water. Drain. Blanch cabbage in boiling water and drain. Brown onion in butter. Add flour and blend. Slowly stir in wine.

Season cabbage and sprinkle with lemon juice. Add cabbage to wine and add sugar. Cover tightly and steam until almost done, about 30 minutes. Add fish and cover with cabbage. Cover and steam for 30 minutes longer. Serves six.

CURRIED
HALIBUT CASSEROLE

2 cups halibut, flaked
1 package (8 oz.) noodles
1 tsp. curry powder
2 tbsp. butter, melted
1/2 cup milk
1 can (10-1/2 oz.) cream of mushroom soup
1 can (1 lb. 4 oz.) asparagus, drained
1 cup grated cheese

❖

Cook noodles as directed on package; drain. Place in a well-greased 2-1/2 quart casserole. Cover with the flaked fish.

Combine curry powder, butter, milk and soup. Pour over fish and noodles. Arrange asparagus over the casserole and sprinkle with cheese. Bake in a moderate oven, 350° for 25-30 minutes or until brown. Serves six.

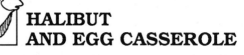

HALIBUT
AND EGG CASSEROLE

2 cups cooked halibut, flaked
2 tbsp. butter
1/2 tsp. salt
Dash of pepper
1 cup milk
1 cup cornflakes, finely crushed
1 hard-boiled egg, chopped
1 tbsp. pimento, chopped
1 tbsp. butter

❖

Melt butter and blend in flour, salt and pepper. Gradually add milk, stirring constantly until thick. Sprinkle half of the cornflakes on bottom of a greased 1-1/2 quart casserole. Arrange halibut, egg, pimento and sauce in layers and top casserole with remaining cornflakes. Dot with butter. Bake at 350° for 25-30 min. Serves four.

HALIBUT CASSEROLE

4 halibut fillets
2 cups chicken broth
4 tbsp. butter
3 tbsp. flour
1/4 cup Dijon-style mustard
1/4 tsp. paprika
Salt and pepper
1 large onion, thinly sliced
1-1/2 lbs. potatoes, boiled
Milk and butter for potatoes
1/4 tsp. grated nutmeg
5 tsp. lemon juice
1/2 cup buttered bread crumbs
1/2 cup grated mild cheese

❖

Poach fish in chicken broth. Remove fillets and reserve broth. Melt 3 tbsp. butter. Stir in flour. Gradually add reserved broth, stirring to make a smooth sauce. Bring to a boil, stirring constantly. Season with mustard, paprika, and salt and pepper to taste.

Saute onion in remaining tablespoon of butter until tender. Mash potatoes with enough hot milk and butter to give a fairly soft consistency. Season with nutmeg.

Butter a shallow baking dish and build layers of half of the fish, half of the onion slices, half of the lemon juice, half of the mustard sauce and half of the potatoes. Repeat layers, ending with potatoes. Sprinkle top with crumbs. Serves four.

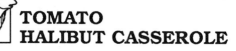

TOMATO
HALIBUT CASSEROLE

1 lb. halibut fillets
1 can whole tomatoes
2 tbsp. onions, minced
1/2 tsp. salt
Dash of pepper
1 tbsp. sugar
Parsley, chopped
1 tbsp. butter

❖

Pour tomatoes in flat baking dish. Sprinkle with onions, salt, pepper and sugar. Place halibut fillets on top of the tomatoes, and sprinkle with a little parsley. Cover and bake in a 350° oven for about 20-25 minutes. Dot with butter before serving. Serves four.

HOT
HALIBUT CREOLE

1 lb. halibut, cut into 1-inch cubes
1/2 onion, chopped
1/2 bell pepper, chopped
2 stalks celery, chopped
2 cloves garlic, finely minced
2 tomatoes, diced
1 (15 oz.) can crushed tomatoes in heavy puree
2 tbsp. dry sherry
1 tbsp. parsley, chopped
1/2 tsp. thyme
1 chili pepper, seeded and chopped

Combine onion, pepper, celery, garlic, tomatoes (fresh and canned), and sherry in saucepan. Simmer until onion becomes clear. Add parsley, thyme, and chili pepper and cook for 2 minutes.

Add fish and allow to simmer for 10 minutes, turning after 5 minutes. Serve over rice. Serves six.

HALIBUT CREOLE

1 pound halibut, cut into 1-inch cubes
1/2 cup onion, chopped
1/2 cup green pepper, chopped
1 clove garlic, minced
1/4 cup butter
1 can (16 oz.) tomatoes, cut up
1 tbsp. dried parsley flakes
1 tbsp. instant chicken bouillon granules
1/4 tsp. bottled hot pepper sauce
1 tbsp. cornstarch
1 tbsp. cold water
Hot cooked rice

❖

Saute onion, green pepper and garlic in butter till tender but not brown. Add undrained tomatoes, parsley flakes, boullion granules, and hot pepper sauce. Simmer, covered, for 10 minutes. Blend together cornstarch and cold water. Stir into tomato mixture. Cook and stir till thick.

Add fish to tomato mixture, stirring to coat. Return to boiling; reduce heat. Simmer, covered, for 5 to 7 minutes or till fish flakes easily when tested with a fork. Serve fish over rice. Serves four.

CREAMED HALIBUT

1 cup cooked halibut, flaked
5 tbsp. butter
3 tbsp. flour
2 cups hot milk
1/2 tsp. salt
1/4 tsp. white pepper
Dash of cayenne pepper
1 tbsp. lemon juice
1 green onion, minced
1/2 cup cooked peas
2 hard-boiled eggs, chopped
1/2 cup bread crumbs

❖

Melt 2 tbsp. of the butter. Stir in flour and cook until bubbly, then beat in hot milk, cooking until sauce thickens and boils.

Remove from heat and season with salt, pepper, cayenne, and lemon juice. Stir in halibut, green onion, peas, and chopped eggs. Pour into a small buttered casserole and top with the remaining 3 tbsp. butter mixed with crumbs. Bake at 350° until the crumbs brown. Serves two.

ARROZ
CON PESCADO

2 lbs. halibut fillets, cut into 1-inch cubes
1/2 cup olive oil
2 large onions, finely chopped
2 cloves garlic, finely chopped
2 cups raw long-grain rice
1 can (1 lb., 12 ozs.) tomatoes
4 cups water
1/4 cup fresh cilantro, chopped
1-1/2 tsp. salt
1/2 tsp. freshly ground black pepper
1/2 lb. shrimp, shelled and deveined

❖

In large pan heat oil and saute onion until tender but not browned. Add garlic and cook one minute. Add rice and cook until rice is lightly browned. Add tomatoes and water. Bring to a boil, cover, and simmer 20 minutes.

Add cilantro, salt, pepper, fish, and shrimp. Push halibut chunks into rice mixture. Cover and simmer until rice has absorbed the liquid. Serves eight.

EASY ARROZ CON PESCADO

1/2 lb. halibut fillets, cut into 1-inch cubes
1/2 cup onion, chopped
1 tbsp. olive or vegetable oil
1 package (6 oz.) curried-rice mix
1 package (about 6 oz.) frozen crab meat,
   thawed and broken in chunks
2-1/2 cups water
1 package (9 oz.) frozen cut green beans

❖

Saute onion in oil just until soft in large skillet. Stir in rice and contents of seasoning packet. Cook, stirring constantly, over low heat just until rice is hot.

Spoon half into a shallow baking dish to cover bottom. Top with half of crab meat and fish. Repeat layers, and arrange seafood attractively on top. Stir water into skillet; bring to boiling; pour over layers in baking dish; cover.

Bake in moderate oven (350°) for one hour, or until rice is tender and liquid is absorbed.

While the seafood bakes, cook beans, and season as you wish. Spoon in a ring on top of seafood and serve. Serves six.

HALIBUT MONTEREY

1-1/2 lbs. halibut fillets
Salt and pepper
1/3 cup dry white wine
Juice of 1 lemon
1 bay leaf, crushed
1/8 tsp. ground ginger
1/4 cup butter
1 tbsp. onion, minced
2 parsley sprigs, chopped

❖

Season fish with salt and pepper. Cut into serving pieces. Roll up the pieces and secure with toothpicks. Put remaining ingredients in a skillet and bring to a boil. Add fish and simmer, covered, for 10 minutes. Serves four.

EASY
CIOPPINO

1-1/2 lbs. halibut, cut into 1-inch cubes
2/3 cup onion, chopped
2 small carrots, sliced
2 tbsp. parsley, minced
1 garlic clove, minced
1/4 cup salad oil
2 tbsp. flour
1/2 tsp. salt
1/4 tsp. pepper
1 can (15 oz.) tomato sauce
2 cups hot water

✜

Saute onion, carrots, parsley, and garlic in hot oil until onion is tender. Remove from heat. Stir in flour, salt, and pepper. Cook over low heat, stirring until mixture is bubbly. Remove from heat. Stir in tomato sauce and water. Cover and simmer 20 minutes. Add fish to sauce. Cover and simmer 30 to 40 minutes. Serves six.

SCALLOPED HALIBUT

1 lb. halibut fillets, cut into 1-inch cubes
2 cups water
1/4 cup onion, chopped
1/4 cup green pepper, chopped
1 tbsp. butter, melted
2 eggs, beaten
1-1/2 cups milk
1-1/2 cups crackers, crumbled
1 can peas and carrots, drained
1 tbsp. lemon juice
2 tsp. Worcestershire sauce
1/8 tsp. pepper
1/2 cup sharp cheese, shredded

✤

Cook halibut in water for three minutes and drain. Saute onion and pepper in butter until tender. Combine eggs, milk and cracker crumbs. Stir in halibut and other ingredients except cheese. Pour mixture into a 2-quart casserole and bake for 50 minutes at 350°.

Sprinkle with cheese and bake five minutes more. Serves six.

CRISPY HALIBUT

1 lb. halibut fillets
1/4 cup lemon juice
1/2 cup mayonnaise
1/2 cup parmesan cheese
2-1/2 cups potato chips, finely crushed

❖

Combine chips and cheese. Set aside.

Combine mayonnaise and 2 tbsp. lemon juice. Dip fish in the other 2 tbsp. lemon juice, then in the mayonnaise/lemon mixture, and then in chip mixture. Arrange in greased baking dish and bake at 375° for 20 minutes or until fish flakes. Serves four.

JACK'S CUBED HALIBUT

1 lb. halibut fillets, cut into 1-inch cubes
1/2 cup peanut oil
1/2 cup cornflake crumbs
1/2 cup bread crumbs
Salt and pepper
Lemon juice

❖

Marinate halibut in lemon juice and spices. Roll cubed halibut in mixture of crumbs. Saute in peanut oil for five minutes or until halibut flakes. Serves four.

CROUTON
BAKED HALIBUT

2 lbs. halibut fillets
1/2 cup mayonnaise
2 tbsp. lemon juice
1 egg, beaten
2 cups seasoned croutons
1 cup corn, drained
1 tomato, chopped
1/4 cup cheddar cheese, grated
2 tbsp. onions, diced
Lemon slices for garnish

❖

Mix mayonnaise, lemon juice and egg. Stir in corn, croutons, tomato, cheese and onion. Spread about two cups of the mixture in a greased baking dish. Place halibut on top of the mixture, and spread the remaining mixture on top of the halibut. Bake at 350° until the halibut flakes (about 50 minutes). Serves six.

HALIBUT KEDGEREE

3 lbs. halibut fillets
1/2 lb. smoked halibut fillet
1 tbsp. oil
1/4 cup butter
1 large onion, chopped
1/2 cup long grain rice
1 tbsp. curry powder
1 tsp. salt
1 can (5 oz.) pimientoes
3 sprigs parsley to garnish
1-1/4 cups boiling water

❖

Poach halibut fillets and smoked halibut in gently boiling water until just tender. Drain and flake. Heat oil and butter and use to saute onion until pale golden. Stir in rice, curry powder and salt. Cook, stirring, for 2 minutes. Add boiling water. Cover and cook until all the water is absorbed.

Chop pimiento, reserving the liquid. Add this to the rice mixture if it becomes too dry. Stir pimiento and flaked fish to rice and heat through. Serve on a warm serving dish and garnish with parsley. Serves four.

EASY
HALIBUT KEDGEREE

2 cups halibut, cooked and flaked
1 tbsp. onion, minced
3 tbsp. butter
2 cups rice, cooked
1/3 cup evaporated milk
1/2 tsp. curry powder
2 hard boiled eggs, sliced
Salt and pepper

❖

Saute onion in butter. Add rice, fish, cream and curry powder. Heat and stir; bring to a boil. Add eggs and season. Serves six.

BAKED
HALIBUT CASSEROLE

1 lb. halibut fillets
1 small can mushrooms
Water
3 tbsp. lemon juice
1/4 cup butter
1/4 cup flour
1/2 tsp. salt
Dash of pepper
2 egg yolks, beaten
2 tsp. finely chopped onion
2 cups green beans and carrots, cooked
1 cup buttered cracker crumbs

❖

Drain mushrooms and save liquid. Combine mushroom liquid, lemon juice and water to make 1-3/4 cups liquid. Melt butter and blend in flour and seasonings. Gradually add liquid, stirring constantly. Cook over low heat until sauce is smooth and thick.

Add a little hot sauce to the egg yolks, then stir egg yolks into rest of sauce. Add mushrooms and chopped onion. Place vegetables in bottom of greased 1-1/2 quart casserole and cover with halibut fillets. Pour sauce over all. Top with buttered cracker crumbs and dot with butter. Bake at 350° until halibut flakes easily. Serves four.

HALIBUT MARENGO

4 halibut steaks
2 large tomatoes, peeled and chopped
1 cup tomato juice
3 oz. mushrooms, sliced (1 cup)
1/2 cup celery, sliced
2 tbsp. onion, chopped
2 tbsp. lemon juice
1/4 tsp. leaf thyme, crumbled
1/4 tsp. white pepper
2 tbsp. parsley, chopped

❖

Place halibut steaks in shallow 2-quart baking dish. Combine tomatoes, tomato juice, mushrooms, celery, onion, lemon juice, thyme and pepper in medium-size saucepan. Bring to boiling. Lower heat; simmer 10 minutes.

Pour sauce over fish. Bake in 375° oven for about 15 minutes or just until fish flakes. Garnish with parsley. Serves four.

HALIBUT
ALMANDINE

2 lbs. halibut fillets
1/2 cup melted butter
Flour, salt, pepper
1/2 cup blanched almonds
2 tbsp. lemon juice
1 can drained peaches

✤

Season flour with salt and pepper. Dip halibut in butter, then in seasoned flour. Place halibut fillets in a greased baking pan and pour the remaining butter over them. Bake at 350° for 20 to 25 minutes, or until fillets flake.

Saute peaches and almonds in butter. Add lemon juice. Spoon a peach and some juice over each fillet. Serves four.

SWEET AND SOUR HALIBUT

4 halibut fillets
1 cucumber, peeled, seeded and cut
  into matchsticks
1 carrot, peeled, and cut into matchsticks
1 sweet pickle, cut into matchsticks
1 tsp. fresh gingerroot, chopped
1/2 cup onion, minced
2 tbsp. salt
2 tbsp. sugar
1/2 cup vinegar
1/2 cup water
4 tbsp. oil
1 tbsp. cornstarch
2 tbsp. soy sauce
2 garlic cloves, minced

❖

Combine cucumber, carrot, pickle, gingerroot, onion, 1 tsp. salt, sugar, vinegar, and 1/2 cup water. Marinate halibut in this mixture for 45 minutes. Remove halibut and reserve marinade.

Place halibut on a rack over 2 quarts salted water and 2 tbsp. oil. Steam fish for 20 minutes, or until fish flakes.

Strain vegetables from marinade and reserve broth. Mix cornstarch and soy sauce into liquid. Saute garlic in remaining oil until brown. Add marinade liquid and cook, stirring until thickened. Return vegetables to sauce and heat. Pour sauce over halibut. Serves four.

FRIED HALIBUT ROLLS

1/2 lb. halibut fillets
1 tbsp. fresh ginger, minced
1/2 tsp. salt
4 slices ham, shredded
1/2 cup raw spinach, shredded
2-3 black mushrooms, soaked and shredded
1 cup flour
1 egg
2/3 cup water
1 tbsp. sesame seeds

✤

Cut fillets into pieces about 4 x 1-1/2 inch. Stuff with mixture of ginger, salt, ham, spinach and mushrooms. Roll and fasten with toothpicks. Combine flour, egg, water and sesame seeds. Dip fillets into batter and deep fry. Serves two.

HALIBUT AND VEGETABLES

1 lb. halibut fillets
1 medium onion, thinly sliced
Salt
1/2 tsp. each: lemon pepper seasoning, dill weed, onion powder
2 small yellow squash, thinly sliced
1 medium zucchini, cut into 2 x 1/8-inch strips
1/4 cup water

Tear off four 12x18-inch sheets of heavy duty aluminum foil. Place onion slices on each sheet of foil. Layer fillets over onion and season with salt.

Combine lemon pepper, dill weed and onion powder; sprinkle half of seasoning mixture over halibut. Dot with half the butter. Place yellow squash slices and zucchini strips over fillets. Sprinkle with water, remaining seasoning mixture and salt. Dot with remaining butter. Wrap in foil. Place foil packets on baking sheet. Bake at 450° for 18 minutes. Serves four.

BAKED HALIBUT WITH FRESH VEGETABLES

1-1/2 lbs. halibut steaks
1 lime or lemon, divided
1 medium carrot, diced
1 stalk celery, diced
4 green onions, chopped
2 tbsp. dry white wine or water
1/4 tsp. oregano, crushed
Salt and coarsely ground pepper
1 medium tomato, peeled and diced
2 tbsp. chopped parsley
1 tbsp. butter

❖

Saute carrot, celery and green onions in butter until tender. Add wine, oregano, dash salt, 1/8 tsp. pepper and tomato; heat thoroughly.

Season halibut with salt and pepper. Place lime slices on steaks and bake at 450° until fish flakes easily. Garnish with parsley. Serves four.

BAKED HALIBUT AND VEGETABLE DINNER

1-1/2 lbs. halibut fillets
3 large potatoes, peeled and sliced thin
1/2 lb. fresh mushrooms, sliced
1 lb. zucchini, cut into 1/8-inch slices
4 large tomatoes, peeled, seeded and sliced
2 green onions, sliced thin
2 tbsp. butter, melted
1 tsp. fresh thyme, chopped, or 1/2 tsp. dried
1 tsp. fresh basil, chopped, or 1/2 tsp. dried
Salt and pepper
Lemon slices to garnish

❖

Arrange potatoes in a two-quart baking dish and sprinkle lightly with salt. Cover with foil and bake for 15 minutes.

Uncover and place mushrooms, zucchini, tomatoes and onions over the partially cooked potatoes. Place fillets over the vegetables. Dribble with melted butter over fish and sprinkle with herbs, salt and pepper. Bake at 350° until halibut is browned and flakes. Garnish with lemon slices. Serves four.

SAVORY HALIBUT SUPPER

1 lb. halibut fillets, cut into 1-inch cubes
4 slices diced bacon.
1 medium onion, sliced
1 cup dry white wine
1 cup water
1 garlic clove, crushed
3/4 tsp. salt
1/4 tsp. pepper
2 medium red potatoes, quartered
1 cup undiluted evaporated milk
3 tbsp. flour
1 tbsp. chopped parsley

✤

Cook bacon in skillet until crisp; remove. Saute onion in drippings. Add wine, water, garlic, salt, pepper and potatoes. Cover. Boil gently 20 minutes.

Add halibut to potato mixture. Boil gently 5 to 10 minutes longer or until fish flakes. Remove halibut and vegetables to platter and keep warm.

Whisk small amount of evaporated milk into flour. Add remaining milk. Stir milk mixture and parsley into skillet. Cook over medium heat, stirring constantly, until mixture thickens. Serve over potatoes and halibut. Garnish with bacon. Serves four.

AK Enterprises Books

Please fill out this form and return to:

**AK Enterprises
P.O. Box 210241
Anchorage, Alaska 99521-0241**

Please send me _____ copies of
Alaska Shrimp and Crab Recipes . . . . $13.95 each

Please send me _____ copies of
Alaskan Halibut Recipes . . . . $13.95 each

Please send me _____ copies of
Salmon Recipes from Alaska . . . . $13.95 each

Please send me _____ copies of
Moose and Caribou Recipes from Alaska . . . . $12.95 each

Total amount for books:	$_____
$1.50 per book for postage/handling	$_____
Total amount enclosed:	$_____

Send books to:

Name: _____

Address: _____

City: _____

State/Zip: _____

Thank you very much for your order. Good cooking!